PLENITUDE

BOOK ONE

CULTURE BY COMMOTION

PLENITUDE

GRANT McCRACKEN

Periph. : Fluide

1997

Such indeed is the diversity, in terms of style, subject matter and geography, that the editors of the New Poetry *could barely find a common link to hold their selection together....*[1] —Times Literary Supplement

In the last fifteen years, French society has become so fluid in certain respects that there has been a sudden, unexpected diversification....[2] —Henri Mendras and Alistair Cole, social scientists

I've spent a lot of time asking myself what it means to be an American musician now. It means finding out everything that's going on in America musically. That's why Cajun music and Texas fiddle are interesting.[3] —Yo Yo Ma, American cellist

[T]he explosion of historical information has led to few new syntheses, few coherent or integrated visions of the past, few organizing frameworks. Rather, reflections ... are more likely to focus upon the splintering, fragmentation, disarray, shapelessness, inaccessibility, incoherence, chaos, anarchy and meaninglessness of it all. [One historian] concludes that "A striking feature of the American historical profession in the last twenty years has been its inability to move toward any overarching interpretation which could organize American, or for that matter, non-American, history."[4] —Philip D. Morgan, American historian

During the last decade, public recognition of national and international differences became an essential internal element of American culture.[5] —Dean MacCannell and Juliet Flower MacCannell, American social scientists

[P]erhaps the immense fragmentation and privatization of modern literature— its explosion into a host of distinct private styles and mannerisms— foreshadows deeper and more general tendencies in social life as a whole.[6] —Frederic Jameson, Professor of Literature and History of Consciousness

[I]nstead of ... the fashion, one is today more likely to see pluralism, with different designers proposing radically conflicting New Looks. While some fashion pundits may strive to reduce this cacophony of different colours, shapes, hemlengths ... into a consistent trend ... anyone viewing the photographs of the Paris, Milan, London or New York shows can appreciate that difference, rather than consensus, is the order of the day.[7] —Ted Polhemus, English sociologist

Whatever narratives or systems that once allowed us to think we could unproblematically and universally define public agreement have now been questioned by the acknowledgment of differences....[8]
—Linda Hutcheon, Professor of Comparative Literature

It's like this puzzle. You spend ages putting things together—things that weren't meant to fit together, disjointed things, things no one would ever think you could put together.[9]
—Tom Rowlands, musician, The Chemical Brothers

I have a sense that in the seventies a great many artists began to do very different sorts of things, not knowing, and perhaps not caring, whether or not it was art... there really was no mainstream in the seventies. Or what looked like a mainstream was countless individual rivulets flowing as one.... The seventies in consequence was a period whose art history is all but inscrutable.[10]   —Arthur C. Danto, philosopher

[T]he world comes to us in pieces, in fragments, lacking any overall pattern....[11]
—Robert Bellah et al., sociologists

[T]he present jumbling of varieties of discourse has grown to the point where it is becoming difficult to label authors ... or to classify works. [This] suggest[s] that what we are seeing is not just another redrawing of the cultural map ... but an alteration of the principles of mapping. Something is happening to the way we think about the way we think.... It is not that we no longer have conventions of interpretation; we have more than ever, [and] a situation at once fluid, plural, uncentered, and ineradicably untidy.[12]
—Clifford Geertz, anthropologist

*Individuality is the most important aspect of beauty today....
Every woman is different.*[13]   —Kathy MacKenzie, fashion editor

The city, Aristotle insists ... is composed of a certain multitude ... but not just any multitude: it must be composed of a multitude that is different in form, eidos,
"for the city does not come into being out of those who are similar."[14]
—Arlene Saxonhouse, political scientist

The appearance of a variety of quite diverse styles [in postwar America]
challenged a central but rarely acknowledged critical tenet that only one
type of art could be valid at a particular time.[15]
—Diana Crane, art historian

What I hope to do is allow people to feel freer about setting tables....
You needn't be worried about mixing your grandmother's china with Pottery
Barn and antiques. If you don't have matching pieces and bought some plates
at the flea market, it doesn't matter.[16]
—Diane Von Furstenberg, designer and arbiter of taste

Now that America is no longer in the forefront when it comes to
industrial and mechanical invention, its job is to produce new cultural types
in what we might call feats of stylistic engineering.[17]
—Margo Jefferson, cultural critic

Utilizing sounds that slide from dub to ambient, jungle to ethnic percussion
and found voices to sci-fi soundbites, [illbient] music reflects the mix of past
and future, the jumble of cultures and the perpetual salvo of sounds and sights
that defines the spectacular intensity of New York City.[18]
—Kathy Silberger, journalist

I'll master your language, and in the meantime, I'll create my own.[19]
—Tricky, musician and an inventor of trip hop

It is hardly possible to overrate the value ... of placing human beings in
contact with persons dissimilar to themselves, and with modes of thought
and action unlike those with which they are familiar.[20]
—Isaiah Berlin, English intellectual historian

We feel affinities not only with the past, but also with the futures that
didn't materialise, and with the other variations of the present that we
suspect run parallel to the one we have agreed to live in.[21]
—Brian Eno, musician and an inventor of Ambient music

For Hargurchet Bhabra, Adrienne Hood, Suzanne Stein
and Wentworth Walker

Periph. : Fluide, Toronto, Canada M5S 2C6

Published 1997
Printed in Canada
2001   2000   1999   1998   5   4   3   2   1

Cataloguing in Publication Data
McCracken, Grant David
   Plenitude
   Volume 1 of the series: Culture by commotion
   Includes bibliographical references
   ISBN 0-9682251-0-1
      1. Culture — popular, contemporary   2. Social Values — Western   3. Pluralism —
anthropological aspects   4. Cultural studies — Canada, U.S., Europe

An electronic version of this book may be downloaded, at no cost, from the webage
www.cultureby.com.
A hard-copy version of this book may be ordered, at cost, from the webpage
www.cultureby.com.
Reader reaction, comment, suggestion, and criticism is particularly welcome.
Please contribute to discussion at the webpage or e-mail the author directly at
grant@cultureby.com.

Culture by Commotion

CONTENTS

Mysteries for Martians

IT'S A DARK AND STORMY NIGHT. We pull our collars up against the autumn chill and quicken our pace. Winter's coming. We just want to get home.

Suddenly the leaves begin to spin in little circles and light fills the sky. A ship sets down beside us. Our presence is requested. We are ushered into the carefully modulated company of an interplanetary other.

There are the usual galactic pleasantries: our planet greets their planet, their planet greets our planet. We are ambassadors to the stars, welcoming our new brethren from beyond. Smiling and nodding, everyone is stupefyingly genial.

Then things seem to run out of gas. If these Martians have an agenda, they're not being entirely clear about it. It's as if they are being ... well ... almost bashful. As if they want to ask something, but can't quite ...

Oh, now it's clear. These Martians want to hear about *themselves*. They want the buzz on Martians. What do we *earthlings* think about them? (Boy, are these guys going to fit in.) The holograms are shimmering with anticipation. The ball's in our court.

Yikes, what *have* we heard about Martians lately?

Well, there was Roseanne on Larry King a couple of weeks ago. She said she's pretty sure she's from outer space. It just explained so much about her. How odd she feels. The things she does. The men she marries. Larry didn't bat an eye. (Is this guy listening?) "Outer space? Let's take a caller from Knoxville, Tennessee."

There's that shimmering thing again and an anxious, whispered conference. (Roseanne, one of us?)

Then there's Frank Black, god of alternative music. Frank believes in creatures from outer space. He contends Area 51 was a giant government conspiracy. Frank is not claiming to be from outer space, but he was "in the presence" once as a child. Frank shares a growing conviction: the truth is out there.

Then there is *Mars Attacks*. Well, *this* is awkward—how do you tell a Martian as image conscious as Edgar Bronfman that he's the butt of Hollywood caricature. (*You* tell him. No, *you* do it!) There is only one truly noble thing to do here. Give up Tim Burton, the director. (Take him, not us!)

And the NASA space probe. We have finally discovered something on the surface of their planet. Ice at the south pole, apparently. The scientists said, that's all we need to make the place habitable; we could live there one day. Well, no, not a permanent installation ... more of a trailer park arrangement, probably. Any time you felt uncomfortable, you could just send in a hurricane. Gone. I believe I speak for everyone when I say, umm, it's your planet. (And all we earthlings merely trailer trash.)

Poof. We're back on the pavement with a "class 1" hangover and the kind of blurred vision you get from optometrist's drops.

At least they didn't kill us ... or remove vital organs. Poking our midsections ruminatively, we trudge home into the dark and the cold with a sense of astonishment. Martians!

What the hell were they after? Ego gratification, possibly. Or *research* — the Martian idea of a focus group. What could Martians learn about us from what we're saying about them? Roseanne, Frank Black, *Mars Attacks*, and a space probe? They're going to stuff this into their thinking machines and get ... what?

Roseanne is a creature to be reckoned with, to be sure. She managed the transition from obscurity to stardom without the usual attributes: beauty, "personality," or the ability to happy talk her way through a *Tonight Show* interview. She came to stardom mostly on the strength of a blistering, fearless candour. And she used what power she had in the early days

to buck the Hollywood system and create television that broke the rules of gender, genre, and television all at once. She gave us a family that was equal parts American, feminist, working class, real life, and lunatic. By all appearances and her own account,[22] she was, in the process, much too intent on celebrity to care very much what anybody thought of her.

Frank Black, on the other hand, appears not to care about celebrity at all. He enjoyed great success a couple of years ago (in a band called the *Pixies*) and then began dismantling his fame stick by stick. He detached himself from a very good recording label (4AD) and now mocks other rock stars (Courtney Love, no less), designs his own astonishingly bad album covers (*Cult of Ray*), subverts or refuses interviews, and generally refuses to play the game. This is a favourite pose of alternative rock ("I never asked to be famous") but Frank appears to mean it. He's navigated the difficult waters from stardom to obscurity with a deft hand and every hope of arrival.[23]

Mars Attacks is Hollywood's latest demonstration that more money doesn't make more movie. For the first time Tim Burton had a huge budget ($70 million) and the results do not impress. The man who appeared to be burning his way through Hollywood may finally have become its captive. This is the man who turned the town on its ear with unprecedented forays into gothic (*Beetlejuice*, 1988; *Edward Scissorhands*, 1990) and camp (*Ed Wood*, 1994). This is the man who was less interested in narrative than the hyperbolically, hypnotically odd (*Batman*, 1989; *Batman Returns*, 1992; *Batman Forever*, 1995). Here finally is a man who appeared to grasp how much audiences now know about moviemaking and was prepared to give them a little credit. So what happened to *Mars Attacks*? It is vacant Hollywood moviemaking: special effects substituting for intelligence, irony unleavened by subtlety, a forced march through popular culture in place of Burton's characteristically brilliant contemplation of it.

And NASA. What an institution this once was! For a society that believed in progress, science, technology, and military prowess, NASA was one of the great shrines of national aspiration. How things change. With ecological crises, and the decline of the authority of science and technology, these days NASA can look like one more player in Washington's budgetary merry-go-round. A nation that once had very deep pockets for the space program must now be cajoled, browbeaten, soft-soaped, and otherwise prevailed upon to come up with even modest funding.[24] A chance to live on Mars? Yawn. The nation could not conceal its lack of enthusiasm. It didn't even bother to try.

They're going to stuff *this* into their thinking machines and get ... what? Good news and bad news. Martians have high-profile spokespeople like Roseanne and Frank Black. In a perfect world, obviously, they would have got Candice Bergen and Liz Phair, but they could have done much worse. (It could have been merely the guy with the tinfoil hat and hand-printed alarms.) From a public relations point of view, *Mars Attacks* left something to be desired. All and all, you'd rather not be cast as a "killer cartoon" and even less as a creature whose head explodes at the sound of Slim Whitman. But this could have been worse, too. (It could have been Walt Whitman.)

But we already suspect there's more to this than press clippings. Chances are these Martians want to know what we think about *them* in order to figure out what they think about *us*. (A kind of "know them as they know you" strategy.) And what might this be? What do we reveal when we think about Martians. When they do an anthropology of the planet using these four observations, what, if anything, will spring to mind?

First, there is *difference* everywhere. Roseanne's comedy bears no resemblance to Frank Black's music. Frank Black's music bears no resemblance to Tim Burton's filmmaking. None has any connection to the world of NASA. They are all the products of the same culture, but they appear to come from (**and represent**) mutually exclusive worlds, each with its own logic, agenda, and point of view. The readout is clear enough: this world is hot and changeable, a house of many mansions, a place of robust diversity and difference. (This is, as it turns out, the topic of *Plenitude*, the first book in the Culture by Commotion series.)

Second, it's a *dynamic* world — everything's in almost constant motion. Roseanne went from being no one to a very big star. Frank Black went from a very big star to the edge of obscurity. Tim Burton has gone from an alternative filmmaker to a mainstream one and from a mainstream hero to a mainstream question mark. NASA has gone from a centrepiece of American culture to something less exalted. New things appear. Then they *transform*. The new renews itself. This world boils. (This is the topic of the second book in the series, *Transformation*.)

There is a final revelation that will issue from the thinking machines. Our culture harbours a genie. Everywhere you look there's an impulse to change, subvert, rethink, redo. Deep within this culture, there is a relentless generative impulse. Roseanne, Frank Black, Tim Burton, NASA — all unthinkable at the middle of the century, and now, at the end, quite taken for granted. Our institutions, our lives, our economies, our cultures have caught a bug. The creative impulse, once the internal resource and privilege of shamans, artists, and visionaries, has escaped into the world and now puts its mark on almost everything. This is the topic of the third and final book in the series, *Commotion*.)

Martian mysteries, to be sure. Or perhaps not so mysterious after all. Perhaps we're "garden variety" in the larger interplanetary scheme of things, something Martians have seen a hundred times before. Somewhere in their textbooks and typologies, there's probably a hard-to-pronounce name for us, a little diagram, and a model that explains us right down to the ground. If we're lucky, one of our Martian friends may someday "share" this wisdom with us. We'll get that exalted piece of e-mail that renders everything perfectly clear.

But for the moment we're on our own. Just you, me, Roseanne, Larry, Frank, Tim, and the space program. God spare us, every one. ❧

Delarue pinx.   Teillard sc.

Plenitude

PLATO, LET'S SAY, RETURNS to walk among us. He becomes, inevitably, a figure of controversy. The talk show circuit demands his presence. ("Today on *Geraldo*: Plato—architect of Western culture or dead white male? You decide!") There are doubts, of course. Production assistants do not warm to elderly men who must be talked out of the wonderstruck examination of a parking meter. ("You're telling me any citizen may make a claim against this space by inserting a coin? That there's an implicit contract between the 'motorist' and other members of the polis?")

But Plato is not *entirely* astonished by the contemporary world. He has seen some aspects of our world before. Indeed, he is familiar with and undaunted by some of the things that puzzle and test us most. He would, for instance, have no difficulty with the blooming, buzzing quality of contemporary life. He wouldn't blink at poetry too diverse for a common theme or fashion dizzy with pluralism.

Plato accepted the world as a place that bloomed and buzzed. He believed diversity was in the very nature of things. What *could* exist, he believed, would exist. Plato's world was driven to complete itself, to fill in every gap.[25] "All that can be imagined must be."

Plato gave us the "principle of plenitude."

> [T]he universe is a *plenum formarum* in which the range of conceivable diversity of kinds of living things is exhaustively exemplified ... no genuine potentiality of being can remain unfulfilled.[26]

There is an important difference, of course. The blooming, buzzing diversity Plato cared about was a property of the natural world. Our diversity is a property of the social world. Plato's diversity is the biodiversity of nature. Our diversity is the plenitude of society. What Plato found astounding was the sheer number of plants and animals in the world. This book is concerned with the sheer number and variety of social species.[27]

But for this difference, a theory of plenitude promises a good deal. It would let us embrace an odd and demanding property of the contemporary world, the sheer profusion and new complexity of social life. As it is, we're frustrated. We're the products of a relatively simple, homogeneous world. We are accustomed to being able to stuff the world into a handful of categories. We used to be able to say, "basically, there are two kinds of people in the world" or to bundle the world into a typology: classes (upper, middle, and working), psychological types (mesomorphs, endomorphs, ectomorphs), birth signs, decades, genders, generations, or life-styles.

mesomorphs,
endomorphs,
ectomorphs

Increasingly, the world won't go along. It overflows even the most agile of our classificatory schemes. We may enjoy a moment's illusion that the world has been restored to order. And then we look around us. Everywhere there is diversity, variety, heterogeneity. And we wonder: What set of categories can comprehend so many species of social life? What typology will embrace the stockbroker in Manhattan, newspaper editor in Vancouver, punk folk singer in Buffalo, small business owner in downtown Baltimore, performance artist in New Orleans, Chinese community leader in Toronto, Brahmin professor in Boston, street person in Seattle, New Age healer in Colorado, skater punk in San Francisco, Gaelic fiddler in the Maritimes, militia member in the Midwest, society leader in Grosse Point, Michigan, community leader in Harlem, francophone separatist in Quebec, Yankee farmer in Maine . . . ?

We can see this in the earnest business of typology construction. Experts are constantly seeking the magic "all but only" formula — the perfect set of categories that will capture all the species out there but only species out there. If the current inflationary pressure is anything to judge by, this is not an easy task. Three categories were once enough to contain the world. The new social inventions made short work of these definitions — overflowing boundaries like the Mississippi on a fine spring day. The experts responded by upping the number of categories to nine. Thus spake the likes of VALS (the Values and Life-Style typology) and Gail Sheehy. Surely these were more than enough to capture and contain the world — but finally they too proved no sturdier than a sandcastle. The experts went back to the drawing board and the number of categories rose to 12 — that'll hold 'em — and already these have been swept away.[28]

A theory of plenitude helps a little. It lets us say, "But of course the world blooms and buzzes with confusion. This is what every contemporary world must do." It soothes classificatory anxieties. It releases us from the anxious hunt for magic new categories that get everything back in the box. Once we assert the new reality, it seems more manageable and less daunting: The world will *always* fill with difference, *no potentiality of being can remain unfulfilled, all that can be imagined must someday be.* There is no box.

anxious hunt

We have seen a great speciation in the last 20 years but to my knowledge we have no survey of it. I want to sketch it briefly, as if from a very great height. I want to show it "all at once" that we may judge just how far the forces of diversity have moved us down the road towards heterogeneity, and what the logic and perimeters of this new imperative might be.[29]

The first readers of this manuscript wanted to know where I stand. Do I think "plenitude" is a good thing? Am I its advocate? Am I "thrilled" it's happening? Yes and no, on all counts. Some plenitude is very good. Some of it frightens me so much I have to put my head between my knees and take deep breaths. Others wanted to know if I have a "vested interest" in plenitude. Do I *need* it to be true? Am I transexual, in the throes of a midlife crisis, keen to be a 13 year old again, caught in new patterns of work, family, life-style, or persuaded I'm an alien? All of these things are no doubt true in their way, especially the alien part, obviously . . . but, no, I don't *need* plenitude to be true. I write this book as an anthropologist, not an advocate.

thrilled

The second purpose is to capture the several factors, conditions, and opportunities that have made plenitude possible. We have thought about this issue surprisingly little. As I will show, the intellectuals have been clumsy and artless on this question — though we will find things of value in the ideas of the postmodernists and the complexity theorists. Political writers have not been much better. The Left has a single explanation (and, for some purposes, it's a good one): the end of hegemony. The Right has another (with its own virtues): the loss of moral compass. But finally these explanations will not do.

Here, then, a quick survey of the new variety of our world. We are accustomed to seeing this in bits and pieces. Yes, we say, gender is now a many-splendoured thing, without seeing that what has happened to gender has happened to every other category in the social world. I want to show all the diversities at once, the better to show the order of magnitude of the change that is upon us.

a many-splendoured thing

A G E

I caught a glimpse of plenitude while doing research in Santa Monica in the spring of 1995. I had set up my video camera on Third Street Promenade and the Santa Monica Pier, and I was asking people to stop for an interview. In California this is more difficult than it used to be. I was greeted with the distaste the new California feels for street people. I was better dressed but not more welcome.

One or two people stopped to talk. One man in particular, a retired engineer who'd worked for the military, said he could give me 10 minutes. (He looked at his watch, an electronic one with lots of fobs, to begin the count.) There was an intensity about him, a high-pitched hum. He dressed as you might expect: heavy glasses, pens in his pocket, everything wash and wear and largely untouched by fashion. I got the feeling that if I gave him 10 minutes and a cup of coffee, he could dash off plans for an irrigation system (for Jakarta *or* L.A.). He was restless and clear-eyed. I wondered whether the hum was momentum.

pens in his pocket

Jerry, let's call him, was in his 70s and becoming a filmmaker. He had no pretensions about this new career. He was not becoming an "auteur" or a "Hollywood" director. He wanted to make "little films." He couldn't tell me exactly what his films were about—he was waiting, he said, for the films to tell him, in the making, the editing, and the viewing. But he was vocal about some of the ideas that drove the project: the clear-eyed wildness of an engineer, his Christianity, a passionate curiosity in the world, the conviction that things were changing and that his camera could capture and provoke this change.

I could hear my stereotypes going off like overheated party balloons. The person, the project, the world were open and emerging. And I was just standing there, caught with expectations built upon stereotypes. By these stereotypes, Jerry was almost impossible to see. His persona parted so completely and unpredictably from my expectations that I could hardly begin to "think" him. He felt like a new species of life, inventing a new species of film.

"Act your age" is no idle admonition in our culture. We were once obliged to follow it precisely. There were specific instructions for the "child," "adult," and "old person." We scripted our performances of the social self accordingly. But something is changing. There are new instructions for "acting your age." A tidy set of categories is coming undone. To be sure, "age instructions" still hold, still shape the lives of North Americans, millions of them, all the time. But everywhere we look we see little acts of refusal.

Seniors

There was a time when "seniors" had particularly clear instructions. "Go quietly" was the important one. "Old" people were expected to remove themselves from the public stage, to relinquish positions of influence and usefulness, to retire their claims to a place at the centre of things.[30]

This is still strong. During the Republican convention of 1996 the comedians were relentless. David Letterman ridiculed Dole, almost nightly. ("Well, it looks like Dole is breathing down Clinton's neck. But, hey, at 92 he's happy to be breathing at all.") This was done "in the best of fun," but if these comments had been about Dole's race instead of his age, Letterman would now be playing checkers with Jimmy the Greek. Some people are more subtle. ("Isn't that sweet. He's retired but he still wears a suit.") Prejudice has a way of sustaining itself; when it can't be prescriptive, it can always be patronizing.

David Letterman

But for all this there has been a quiet revolution among the elderly. Many *won't* go quietly. (In the culture of commotion, fewer do.) They are throwing off stereotypes. There may come a time when "old" people will be as diverse and heterogeneous as those of middle age.[31] It looks increasingly as if people who were once relieved of their selfhood as they crossed the threshold of 70 will insist on taking it with them as they go.[32] One of them told me, "I want to live for myself and not worry quite so much what the neighbours think." In the words of Florida Scott-Maxwell, "Near the end of my life I am myself as never before."[33] Anthropologically, it is hard to know exactly what this means. But it's clear being "oneself" takes the individual away from, not towards, the conventional "age instructions" of our culture.

If there *is* a larger movement away from orthodoxy, one thing is clear. In the culture of commotion, "old age" may well become an open category, a licence to become the person one could *not* be in middle age. What used to be a "greying station," where individuality was rinsed away, may become a staging ground for transformation.[34]

The structural implications take the anthropological breath away. The "later" years would become *more* rich and diverse than the middle and junior ones. Seniors would become *more* various and expressive than their conformist, predictable juniors. It's possible that Jerry is one of those odd creatures that California has been throwing off for decades. He may be a delirious act of invention that promises nothing, predicts nothing, presages nothing. On the other hand...

Teens

I studied teens seven years ago.[35] An ardent TV viewer, I expected, vaguely, to find myself talking to the likes of Alex P. Keaton, the character played by Michael J. Fox in *Family Ties*. But in 1990 Alex P. Keaton existed only on TV.[36] The "preppie" teen was disappearing. In his place was a world teeming with diversity. I went to the mall and asked a local teen to help identify the new species of social life.

"So what's he?" I asked.
"Ah, he's a rocker. You know, heavy metal music."
"And him?"
"He's kind of a surfer-skater kind of guy."
"And those girls?"
"Oh, man, those are b-girls."

"What about her ... and her?"

My informant turned to gaze at me in wonder that anyone could be so thoroughly stupid.

"She's a goth and that's a punk."[37]

By the time I had finished the study, I could manage without a "seeing eye" companion. There were some 15 types of teen. Once more the anthropologist finds himself with his stereotypes showing. Nothing in my experience as a teen, nothing in the academic literature, had prepared me for this. The category "teen" is itself a relatively recent invention, and for a long time it was structurally simple, containing relatively few choices. In the 1950s, for instance, there were only two categories of teen. As one respondent put it, "When I was 16, you could be mainstream or James Dean. That was it. You had to choose."[38] Without much fanfare, we got more complicated.

b-girls, goths, punks, and skaters

But this is just one half of plenitude. We are not just talking about *lots of differences*. We are talking about differences with depth. As I began to talk to b-girls, goths, punks, and skaters I found myself listening to dramatically different values, outlooks, points of view. Differences of fashion, clothing — the differences of the surface — turned out to indicate differences below, differences of value and perspective.

The experts sometimes keep us from seeing the depth of these differences. Some say teens are driven by "peer group acceptance." What counts, they say, is the consuming insecurity of the life-stage. Hairstyles, clothing choices, speech patterns, leisure choices, music preferences — these are just so many fads and fashions — high school's sound and fury, as it were, signifying nothing, brute coinage every teen must pay to belong.

A second camp has another way of concealing the depth of differences. It insists that the robust and vigorous diversity of the teen world comes down to one thing, the same thing. All these new styles of self-presentation, activity, and outlook are really the expression of age and class hostilities. Teens are being transgressive.[39]

In both cases, we wish away what's going on. And what's going on is astonishing. The surface commotion of the teen world comes from a deeper, more systematic process of innovation that is throwing off a variety of types of teen, each with its own ideas, values, and ideologies. These types are well defined, easily read, consistently maintained, and policed with some vigour. Were peer pressure or protest the real cause of teen plenitude, none of this would be necessary, all of it would be gratuitous.[40]

Consider these ethnographic particulars. *Hippies* of the 90s, like those of the 60s, have a preference for the rural and the natural, for the spiritual and the uncontrived, for the spontaneous gesture and an egalitarian generosity. This is a well-defined, highly consistent set of values. *Rockers* refuse virtually all of this. At their worst, rockers are preoccupied with domination and a hostility for anything different, foreign, or unknown, and make the lads in *This Is Spinal Tap* look like men of taste and learning.[41] This music is "headbanging," anthemic, and tribal where hippie music is spiritual, questing, and delicate.[42] Here, too, "look" is "language," a statement of a particular view of the world.

B-boys and girls are, in a sense, rockers reinvented in the style of the American ghetto and changed in the process. B-boys play out, embrace, the violence of the street. They cultivate the preemptive visual strike, the show of gang menace, the declaration of a toughness of which the rocker can only dream and the hippie only dread. More to the point, the b-boy/girl ideology is a response to the particular conditions of racism and poverty in the ghetto and therefore crafted in, and for, cultural circumstances unlike anything known to the rocker or the hippie.[43] This is a rich and coherent worldview.

Goths are preoccupied with introspection and melancholia. They are inclined to speak poetically of "beautiful deaths" and vampiric sympathies.[44] Theatrical as they are, goths are not (or not only) play-acting and self-dramatizing. There is a coherent, defined, and engaging worldview, one that summons otherworldly forces and creatures that have no place at all in the cosmologies of the hippie, rocker, or b-boy. With dark cloaks, died black hair, and heavy eyeliner, this community of teens does not merely look different from other teens, it is giving voice to its own distinct cultural universe.

Punks are, by one reckoning, the Asian monks of our society. At their best, they have renounced the bourgeois world in order to instruct the rest of us in the deceptions of desire and the illusory nature of the material world. Punks will tell you they use homemade tattoos and body piercings to jolt the rest of us out of the prisonhouse of our conformity. They break rules in order to reveal rules.[45] There is a nihilism here that would horrify the hippie, stun the rocker, puzzle the b-boy, and repel the goth. But it is well-formed nihilism and a world unto itself.

In each of these cases, we are looking at deep cultural completion and something much more than superficial differences. Each of these groups represents what I would call, for want of a better term, a "little culture." True, many of these groups engage in protest, but what is interesting is how different (and internally coherent) each protest is. To explain all these teen subcultures as the same act of protest is to generalize just when we need to be particularizing. It is to sacrifice the ethnographically illuminating for the glib larger truth.

Let me acknowledge that teens will often belong to more than one culture, that they will move from culture to culture in time and over time, and that they will even "mix and match" these styles from time to time. But let us also note that this is not the postmodernist's *pastiche*. There are basic types of teen. They remain coherent and habitable, with characteristic values, practices, and styles. We do not (yet) live in a world in which each teen invents himself by inventing new cultural and aesthetic resources. When mixing and matching takes place, it is always the mixing and matching of preformed materials. (In another language, in the language of linguistics, morphemes come, as morphemes must, prefab.[46]) "Oh, man, those are goths," is still a possible, frequent, and necessary act of recognition.[47]

This is the most cursory of reviews, but it is perhaps enough to show two things. First, that the world of teens is simply exploding with difference. And, second, that the culture of commotion is doing something more than simply throwing off variety. It is generating deeper cultural types, each its own reckoning of the world, each an entire culture in little, carrying its own view of the world. If the surface difference is impressive, this deeper difference is simply breathtaking. Generally cultures do not do this. They are designed in fact to keep this from happening. Plenitude is a strange and powerful virus.

What a world plenitude is making. And we have talked only about the synchronic diversity—all the diversity that exists right now. The diachronic diversity—diversity over time—expands the possibilities dizzyingly. We have for some decades lived in a culture where generations are said to occupy something like their own cultures. But we are seeing something finer in the works. Someday we may have to think in terms of half-decades and even two-year cohorts. Is there a natural limit here? Someday will we need to know the *year* someone came of age to understand the forces that shaped them. The logic of plenitude appears to run both synchronically and diachronically. And it appears to have no natural point of closure. It will continue to divide us more finely and more deeply.

So much for the "seven ages of man." At one end of the age continuum, teens show new diversity and depth of difference. At the other, the elderly are creating a profusion of their own. I will not examine the remaining categories (childhood, early adulthood, middle adulthood), but perhaps I have said enough to suggest that this entire "system of difference" (as the structuralist would call it) is becoming precisely that. It is a system that throws off difference. Teens now teem. The elderly teem. The whole team teems, one and all.

GENDER

Straights

Gender and sexuality have "speciated" dramatically in the postwar period. A culture that was prepared to "certify" a handful of male and female identities now plays host to many of them. If Hollywood stars are a reliable map, we live in an increasingly diverse world. To begin with the heterosexual world, even the most obtuse observer would acknowledge that Alan Alda, Spike Lee, Johnny Depp, Tim Allen, Lyle Lovett, Prince, Woody Allen, and Sylvester Stallone represent different but equally accepted styles of masculinity. Our culture once had many fewer ideas on the topic of masculinity (James Stewart, John Wayne, and James Cagney, say). Roseanne, Madonna, bell hooks, Dolly Parton, Fran Drescher, Kate Moss, Diane Sawyer, Bjork, and Winona Ryder represent different but plausible female styles. Once we made do with Barbara Stanwyck, Ava Gardner, and

Spike Lee

Donna Reed. The culture that once policed gender with vigilance is newly forgiving (and productive) of diversity.

This florescence has many causes. One of the most important is the rising conviction that biology is *not* destiny. This notion is not uncontested, and hardly a month passes when we do not hear of research from the laboratory that biology *is* the basis of gender. But there is a large and restless movement towards skepticism on this score, and the break with biological determinism has had extraordinary effects. It says, there is no "natural fact" of femaleness or maleness. Behaviour is not the inevitable playing out of biological imperatives but a cultural "performance."[48] In this manner of speaking, gender is really genre, a set of conventions for constructing and performing the self. Butler argues that, in our culture, there's so little connection between the public definition of women and the "natural" facts of the matter that women are obliged to engage in a "persistent impersonation," that they must, in effect, pretend to be "women."[49]

As feminism explores the world of possibility it has opened up, the number of habitable versions of "being female" is exploding. If we may return to media personalities once more, it is interesting that there are at least five very different female characters visible on network TV. Cybil, Grace, Caroline, Roseanne, and Ellen are all, relatively speaking, powerful, forthright women, but all are quite different in their construction of the self. Women have succeeded in appropriating professional identities once reserved for men: Mafia crime boss, city politician, sports celebrity, etc. But they have also explored possibilities unanticipated in the male domain, especially in the realm of healing and direct marketing (e.g., midwives in the first case, Martha Stewart in the second).[50] These new possibilities deliberately challenge and undo the conventions of the male domain. Thus does plenitude expand.

Martha Stewart

As new categories of femaleness emerge, old categories are refurbished. The recently published *The Rules: Time-Tested Ways for Capturing the Heart of Mr. Right* encourages women to return to the most conventional definitions of gender.[51] One of the authors says, "The Rules are a way of behaving with men which makes them want to marry you." The most important rule: Play hard to get. Rule 17: Let him take the lead.[52] Plenitude never opens up the new without

hard to get

refurbishing the old. There is almost always a "rebound" effect. In this case, new species of femaleness provoke the affirmation of old species of femaleness.

"Maleness" is undergoing its own florescence. To the extent gender categories traditionally have been mutually defining, this does not surprise us. (But now rebound is happening across genders, not just within them.) There are two structural possibilities. As above, new categories of femaleness have prompted some to refurbish *old* categories of maleness. This tendency shows most spectacularly in the work of Robert "Iron John" Bly. It is also evident in the *Promise Keepers* movement, founded in 1990 to restore traditional gender relations and to demonstrate that a "man's man is a Godly man."[53]

There are also, inevitably, *new* categories of maleness. A body of academic and ideological work applies the insights of feminism to reinvent "maleness."[54] Characteristics once thought intrinsic to the beast (aggression, competitiveness, individualism, etc.) are being questioned and reframed. The influence of feminism aside, there are several factors that would reshape maleness. Consider, for instance, the therapeutic and New Age challenge of the Type A (read "masculine") personality.[55] Thus does a culture that once insisted on one or two acceptable versions of masculinity see the emergence of many of them.

But this only begins to map the diversity of the gender domain. After centuries of covert existence, the categories "gay" and "lesbian" have established themselves as incontrovertible (though not uncontroversial) realities of the social world. As *categories*, these show on the "radar" of even the most backward and hostile North American. At a stroke, our *mainstream* gender categories have doubled. They have done so in a decade or two.

America suddenly found itself living alongside a homosexual second society, a segregated parallel social world that had sprung up in every large city and many smaller ones, that involved several million men and women, hundreds of organizations, and billions of dollars' worth of businesses. By 1980 the United States and Canada had acquired the largest, best-organized, and most powerful homosexual minority in the history of the world.[56]

Gays and Lesbians

The gay world *represents* plenitude — it doubles our gender categories. And it *promotes* plenitude — new styles of gayness emerge continuously. Esther Newton observed, for instance, how the *sissy* style was supplanted by the *clone* and *leather* looks in the New York city of the late 1970s:

leather looks

> Where ten years ago the streets of Greenwich Village abounded with limp wrists and eye makeup, now [circa 1977] you see an interchangeable parade of young men with cropped hair, leather jackets and well trimmed mustaches. [There has been] a proliferation of ersatz cowboys, phony lumberjacks and (most sinister) imitation Hell's Angels, police and even storm troopers.[57]

phony lumberjacks

On the West Coast, *sissy* was supplanted still more vigorously.

> [G]ay styles were proliferating, becoming more various. That is, while the Castro [a neighbourhood in San Francisco] presented a fairly uniform look to outsiders, its denizens could point out a huge number of species and subspecies, each as distinct as warblers. There was the clone style proper: short hair, clipped mustache, blue jeans, and bomber jackets. There was the preppie-athletic look: Lacoste or rugby shirts and well-shined loafers. There was the cowboy look, the logger look, the bodybuilder look, and so on.... What was surprising was not that these varieties of dress existed but rather that the wearers did not seem to mix any more than did warbler species.[58]

In this case, plenitude has a method. *Sissy* comes to be seen as a capitulation to straight stereotypes (gay male as weak and incapable): it must be repudiated. There emerges a new look, a hypermasculinity, and the community expands. The Village People, the band created by Jacques Morali in 1977, were a deliberate survey of the possibilities: American Indian, cowboy, policeman, construction worker, biker, soldier.

The Village People

But there is a dynamic within the dynamic. As Foucault pointed out, certain acts of protest may validate the very categories from which escape is sought.[59] From this point of view, both *sissy* and *clone* were seen to be problematical for they reproduced gender categories instead of reinventing them. No sooner had hypermasculinity been asserted than the community began to investigate gender styles unanticipated by the straight world. Thus does plenitude renew itself.

In the AIDS era, *leather* and *clone* styles have been muted and transmuted, and they are now to some extent supplanted by the "boy movement" and several varieties of "mature gay" style and even gay skinheads.[60] Traditional styles, like *drag*, change; others, like *cholorap*, emerge. Further changes are at hand as new ethnic groups enter the community, the Metropolitan Community Church continues to grow, and as coffeehouse and restaurant supplement (and compete with) the bar scene as social centres of the community.[61] Gayness continues to be both the product of plenitude and one of its engines.

cross talk

The gay community is not an island. "Cross talk" means gay innovations routinely shape straight gender.[62] When, as we have seen, the gay community becomes a *producer* of gender identities rather than the consumer of existing ones, the straight community has access to a new source of innovation. The movement of gender innovations between the straight and gay communities is the very stuff of plenitude.

butch

In the lesbian community, there is diversity as well.[63] As Kennedy and Davis point out, this diversity begins with the "butch" and "femme" distinction of the traditional lesbian couple, a diversity deepened by the influence of class and race.[64] These "pre-revolutionary" gender identities live on in the feminist era, where, increasingly, they admit of shifting interpretations. In a sense, the "transgressive" inclination of the community has been turned upon the community itself.[65]

lipstick lesbian

The diversity within the lesbian world now supports at least three quite different communities. One of these is the community that created and defined itself through the Michigan Womyn's Music Festival. The telling stylistic signature of this community is captured in the terms used sometimes to describe it: "crunchy granola," "Birkenstock brigade,"[66] and "unicorn and waterfall set." There is a second community created and defined by the Dinah Shore Golf Tournament, sometimes characterized by the term "lipstick lesbian" or "lesbian chic." This may be a reflection of a "hyperfemininity" movement, which parallels the hypermasculinity development noted in the male gay community. Finally, there is a younger community, still more diverse in trends, styles, and codes — some alternative, some mainstream.[67]

There is opportunity for speciation within each community, for each community sustains values and perspectives that can fracture it. Working without the benefit of long-standing conventions, rituals, and agreed-upon practices, each community must define itself as it goes along. Inevitably there are diverse ways of executing these values, and therefore there is always opportunity for fission, breakaways, and innovation.[68]

Until very recently the transformational activities of the gay and lesbian communities have taken place *sub rosa*, far from the gaze of the straight community. But as gay and lesbian communities prove more active and visible (and for all the present political alarm, they *are* that), more and more of this transformation takes place in the public domain. When this occurs, opportunities for "cross talk" amplify. The growing influence of a gay sensibility on the television situation comedy is perhaps telling.

> There are openly gay and lesbian writers on almost every major prime-time situation comedy you can think of, including *Seinfeld, Murphy Brown, Roseanne, Mad About You, The Nanny, Wings, The Single Guy, Caroline in the City, Coach, Dave's Friends* and *Boston Common....* even the most heterosexual of sitcoms possess an undertone of "gay sensibility" — *Frasier* being a case in point.... In a way, all the episodes of these shows are gay.[69]

It counts for something that gay and lesbian communities are no longer so systematically excluded from, defamed in, or patronized by the media. Mainstream actors play gay characters, as Tom Hanks did in *Philadelphia* and Glenn Close did in the NBC movie *Serving in Silence*.[70] As Vito Russo aptly points out, real inclusion happens only when a character's gayness is incidental to the plot instead of its preoccupation.[71] But plainly there is some movement. The industry standards that forced Rock Hudson to "pass" as a heterosexual are changing a little. David Geffen and Harvey Fierstein no longer engage in this impersonation. One of the executive producers of *Friends* says, "I've been called 'David-Crane-openly-gay-producer' so often, it's virtually become one word."[72] Another milestone: Ellen DeGeneres's doppelganger "Ellen" came out on national television, April 30, 1997.

Gay rock and roll stars have always been franker than their Hollywood counterparts and more visible. Gender bending is a long-standing feature of the rock and roll stage persona and part of the star's charisma.[73] But there are now stars who are unambiguously gay or lesbian: Elton John, Melissa Etheridge, and k.d. lang (and the lesser known Tribe 8, God Is My Co-pilot, Pansy Division, and Imperial Teen).[74]

Pansy Division

All of these are important developments in the world of plenitude. When the entertainment industry ceases to "enforce" gender stereotypes, it becomes a test bed for their innovation.

Transgenderists

But there are perhaps still more sexual categories in the works. *Transgenderists* identify not with the gender of their birth but the one of their choice. There are "male to female" and "female to male" transgenderists. Some undergo surgery and/or hormonal therapy. Others argue these "remedies" are unsafe, unsuccessful, and unnecessary and, what's worse, that they defer to the mainstream conviction that sex and gender must be congruent, that you must be bodily constituted as a woman (or man) to act like one.[75]

It is not clear whether transgenderists create *new* categories of gender. Certainly, many wish merely to give up one gender identity and assimilate to another one. To this extent, they are switching categories, not inventing them. However, a recent issue of the *Village Voice* shows transgenderists seeking one another out and this suggests the possibility that they are not "migrating" between gender categories but establishing their own.[76] Garber has argued they have created a "third term."[77]

But the transgenderist movement is important for other purposes. It contributes to a rethinking of sex and gender. The transgenderists demand the reexamination of cultural assumptions. And they challenge some of our most deep seated and otherwise inscrutable ideas. Most significantly, they insist on a radical *delinking* of culture and biology. Biology, they say, has nothing to do (necessarily) with sexuality, sexuality nothing to do (necessarily) with gender, and gender nothing to do (necessarily) with identity.[78] In sum, they push the feminist attack on "natural gender" a step further still.[79]

Bornstein, for instance, refuses the following "rules of gender":

1. There are only two genders
2. These genders are assigned by nature and invariant
3. Genitals (and hormones) are the essential indicator of gender
4. There is no movement between genders except by ritual events such as masquerade[80]

Bornstein's skepticism may have no direct influence on the mainstream community. But the indirect influence is unmistakable. It is clear, for instance, that Madonna draws upon transgenderist fashions and ideologies. When she made "voguing" the fashion of the moment, she was borrowing liberally from the transgenderist community. By this and other means, the transgenderist challenge works its way into our culture.

How much variety has plenitude created in the gender world? We have no way of mapping all the categories that exist there. But there *guy seeks gal* are crude measures. Consider these sexual identifiers from ads in the the *Village Voice*: SWF, SBM, MWM, BiPRM, GAM, GHF, SBJF, MWBi, BiSWM, Pre-op TS, SHM, SWJM, MBiHCpl, ISO, and GBMPRM.[81] So much for the monochromatic simplicities of "guy seeks gal."

Gender teems as teens do. Where once there were, officially, two basic categories, male and female, now there are many gender identities. There are now at least eight: straight male, straight female, gay male, gay female, transgenderist (male to female), transgenderist *spivak* (female to male), neuter, and spivak. (These last two are choices devised by and for participants of the virtual chat lines on the Internet.[82]) If we add the vast speciation that is taking place *within* each of these categories, the number is much higher. By this reckoning, we may now have as many as 42 kinds of gender.[83] There are more to come — perhaps many more. As Baudrillard puts it in his characteristically breathtaking way, "Pushed to its logical conclusion, this would leave neither masculine nor feminine, but a dissemination of individual sexes referring only to themselves, each one managed as an independent enterprise."[84]

STYLES OF LIFE

slackers New species of social life form everywhere in the culture of commotion: around a football team (e.g., Raiders fans), a rock group (e.g., Deadheads), a TV series (e.g., Trekkies), a leisure activity (e.g., line dancing), an economic downturn (e.g., slackers), an economic upturn (e.g., preppies), a means of transport (e.g., Hell's Angels), a modernist aesthetic (e.g., space-age bachelor-pad music), a sports activity (e.g., Ultimate Frisbee), a movie (e.g., *Rocky Picture Horror Show*), and a communications technology (e.g., geeks).[85]

Apparently almost anything can serve as a rally point. And this tells us the sheer potential for plenitude. There are, after all, a great many sports and many teams within each sport, a very large number of rock groups, TV series and leisure activities in the hundreds, and defining economic events at least once a decade. If any of these can give rise to a new species of social life, the options are quite remarkable. Age and gender may teem with new diversity, but they cannot begin to compare to life-style. This may be the "Burgess shale" of the new Cambrian explosion, a place of particular fecundity.[86]

Once more, this innovation is not fad or fashion. Doubters may try a simple test: tell a Raiders fan they are posturing. Tell them how much they have in common with Jean-Paul Gaultier. This sensibility is hard-bitten, cynical, openly hostile to middle-class niceties. It is the working-class answer to the playing grounds of Eton. Sport ceases to

Raiders be a place of "honourable" conduct and becomes a bloodying refusal of hypocrisy. Raider passion shapes the way these individuals think of themselves as parents, workers, community members, children of God, and citizens of the state. "Raiderness" is thoroughgoing and it goes deep. It is a "little culture."

"Life-styles" supply detailed life instructions. I have listened to Trekkies mapping out the starship *Enterprise* as if it were not a virtual space but a real one (and this well before the appearance of "ship's manuals" on CD-ROM). But it is equally clear that this TV program has long provided navigational coordinates for moral space as well. Decisions are made routinely in our culture on the basis of what Captains Kirk or Picard would do. There are people who understand themselves better because of Data's attempts to understand himself.

There is extraordinary breadth. The Raiders fan and the Trekkie could hardly have less in common. Line dancers and Hell's Angels might as well come from different galaxies. Geeks and Deadheads are on many points unrecognizably different. This speciation has been as extensive as it's been intensive.

The fourth point, one some readers will have been awaiting with interest, is that each of these life-styles is something more than the precipitate of the general culture. It is also a *maker* of the culture. Certainly, there are shared values at work here. These groups do not invent themselves *de novo* and they do not exist in isolation. But they do create their own, highly distinctive configurations of cultural meaning. The life-style of the Hell's Angels is made up of meanings we see elsewhere and on which other groups draw. But these meanings take on a particular character in their hands. In T.S. Eliot's turn of phrase (and has it ever been used more appositely?) these creatures are not borrowing, they are stealing.[87] The gendered, classed, and "outlawed" meanings they draw from the general culture are transformed by the configuration into which they enter in the Angels format—and when they return to the general culture, they help to change it.

T.S. Eliot

And, yes, we can say that space-age bachelor-pad music is "camp" of a conventional kind and that it draws heavily on one of the "gay" aesthetics. But we cannot say it is merely derivative. Camp is changed in the new context and it is returned to the general culture with qualities, depths, subtleties and executions it did not have before. When Richard Linklater directed the generation-defining film *Slacker*, he drew on techniques and strategies from the history of film. But as he deployed these techniques and strategies, they took on and gave off more particular meanings (for a film and a life-style).

It turns out that everything's a sunken ship. This was the great surprise of the North Sea oil platforms. When they weren't spilling and leaking, it turned out they did not damage sea life but helped it flourish. With a platform in place, an empty sea bed suddenly came alive. This holds true for most of our "contributions" to the marine world, especially sunken ships. We lose them only to discover a few weeks later they've become a habitable world for every kind of sea life.

And so it is in the social world. Anything can be a sunken ship — a point around which a species of social life can muster. But, strictly speaking, the metaphor has its limits. After all, real sunken ships draw only existing species while the metaphorical ones of the contemporary world actually help invent new ones. But why reach for such outlandish comparisons when we have a simpler one at hand? Consider the magazine rack. These were once paltry affairs with room for 10 or 12 titles. The number has grown steadily in the last few years, a positive florescence, until now any self-respecting rack has several hundred species swimming in and out of it.

sunken ships

The notion of *life-style* is itself a creation of plenitude. It was devised by social scientists precisely because existing typologies could not contain the diversity of the social world. The idea of *class*, long the great principle of explanation, proved less and less useful. It was harder and harder to find reliable consistencies of education, activity, income, ownership, outlook. Some elites had power but no ownership. Blue collars were sometimes more prosperous than white. The individual's class origins predicted less and less of their eventual class destination. Occupational prestige was sometimes widely at variance with education, income, and power. The world would not line up.[88]

by Commotion

The idea of life-style proved more supple. Unlike the theory of class, it did not specify in advance the content, logic, or origins of a life-style. It said merely that certain backgrounds, activity, incomes, and outlooks would go together in consistent little bundles (that they would travel in packs) and that when they did, the social scientist could pin them to her board. Hey, presto, with this new set of lenses, life-styles could be seen in great number.[89]

The idea of life-style solved one problem only to create another. If class captured too little, life-style captured too much. It cast the net too wide. It let in the sheer fecundity of the world — and did nothing to diminish it. The results were stunning. Not only were there a lot of "life-styles" out there, they were coming and going at an astonishing rate. To observe them all at once was to draw near to the precipice of social scientific understanding. It was to canvass how much there is, and how little we know. For analytic purposes, "life-style" proved more a confession of ignorance than a theoretical advance.

MONSTERS

Plenitude produces many new species of social life, and some of these are truly monstrous. Paramilitary groups, in the person of Timothy McVeigh, have unleashed their horror. Skinheads and White Power groups are visible in every Western city.[90] The burning of African American churches is epidemic in parts of the U.S. Anti-Semites and the so-called Aryan Nation are active and voluble, attacks on synagogues not uncommon.[91] Anti-gay groups engage in systematic acts of violence, sometimes with the tacit support of an organized church.

But it is not just the radical right that throws off these monsters. We have lived for some time with the Bloods and the Crips in one community, Hell's Angels in another. These groups may be somehow institutionalized, traditional, almost "part of the woodwork," as it were. But this does not make them less monstrous. Gangs are agents of malice and misery that have, very much in the Platonic scheme, found a place to live in the spaces between other, undegraded, species.

Cults and sects are equally bewildering. Some, like the Moonies, appear relatively benign but mark, in any case, an extraordinary departure from many of the conventions of the social world. Others, as in the case of Charles Manson's cult, are plainly malevolent and frightening. There are groups so implacably opposed to the existing order that they are prepared to risk the fate of David Koresh's Branch Davidians rather than defer to the authority of government institutions. And then there are groups so removed from our reckoning of the world that mass suicide presents itself as the appropriate course of action (e.g., Jonestown, Guyana, Solar Temple, Heaven's Gate).[92]

Cultu

Charles Manson

The conditions that allow for the efflorescence of new species of gender and age also allow for the rise of species driven by hatred, violence, or just plain strangeness. Not all of these monsters are new, to be sure. The world has endured racists and anti-Semites from the beginning of recorded history. But it is clear that the groups that once existed in the shadows, constrained by the hegemonic powers of the mainstream, are bolder and more visible.[93] In a world open to and encouraging of new species of life, it is much harder to dissuade these groups of their right to exist and to proselytize. We could once bring resounding social, intellectual, and/or moral authority against them. But we are now so decentred and so numerous in the mainstream, the margin admits of less control.

But it is clear that these groups *are* "species," and not merely ideological or aesthetic inclinations. Skinheads have characteristic manners of speech, dress, music, and association as well as objective, outlook, and worldview. These are "little cultures" with precisely the power to claim the individual in broad, general ways and fine, particular ones. The ability of each species to resocialize its members, drawing them away from the mainstream into the cultivation of alternative ideas, is clear and it may well be growing. Plenitude is not just creating monsters, it is creating robust ones.

skinheads

It is hard for the rest of us to imagine what it would take to persuade us to give up lives and careers, and take our families to armed compounds in the countryside. But paramilitary groups are now so compelling they can effect precisely that. The U.S. has always been a culture capable of creating cults that will suddenly take their leave of the mainstream. But has something changed? Cults once demonstrated their marginality when they moved. Everyone, including would-be recruits and sympathizers, understood that in taking leave of the body politic these individuals were taking leave of their social credentials and credibility. It's not clear this still happens. In some cases, both the cult and its wider circle have no sense of forsaken membership. Indeed, for some, marginality is a kind of proof of their position. Were their position not so just, they would not feel it so intensely.

Plenitude has created and encouraged speciation. It has done so in a relatively dispassionate manner, inventing the bad with the good.

We would be wrong to think of it as a "force for good," however much good it accomplishes. It has invented monsters and it will continue to do so.[94]

TIME

Western societies have a peculiar attitude towards time. "Traditional" societies seek repetition and return. Generally, time is round. Western ones seek difference and departure.[95] Generally, time's an arrow. This is always an extraordinarily complicated cultural artifact, and in the Western case, it is especially so — because one of the things that change as a result of the Western concept of time is, of course, the Western concept of time. There are, in the postmedieval period, early modern, Renaissance, industrial, modernist, and electronic versions of time, and the topic admits of extraordinary complexity.[96]

But if there is something *shared* in the Western concept in the postmedieval period, it is the notion that time is open. This is what Levi-Strauss meant when he called ours a "hot" society.[97] We are, he said, constantly seeking after "that other message." We are prepared to live in a world in which the "now" and the "next" are at odds. We are capable of enduring a world where we really have no idea what the future holds. We are accustomed to having to "let go" of the moment in order to "remain on board" the present.

Naturally, this makes for a tumultuous world and one very large problem. How *do* we get everyone to "let go" and move on? And when they do, how do we get them to move in the same direction — and come to rest in the same place? How, in short, do we manage the wagon train, bringing up stragglers and holding back the ones inclined to ride off in all directions. This has been one of the miracles of the contemporary world, that we are all changing, but somehow, all changing, more or less, in the same way, at the same rate, in the same direction.

One of our solutions has been to construct "temporal cultures." It is to say, in effect,

For the purposes of this time-period (e.g., century, decade, year, season) we shall allow the emergence and insist upon the adoption of a certain constellation of cultural values, which constellation shall *not* be binding in perpetuity but will hold only until a *new* temporal culture is declared and a new constellation of cultural values allowed to emerge. This constellation shall have the individual's attention and loyalty — until he/she is obliged to forsake it and move on.

It's a dizzying thing from an anthropological point of view — much more contingent, temporary, and fragile than the usual stuff of ethnographic investigation. But it seems to work well enough. The great advantage of the temporal culture is that it allows order in the disorder. Vast groups of people can embrace novelty without, necessarily, parting company. Change does not have to be the end of consensus. We are able, finally, to keep the wagons together.

The temporal cultures we know best are the ones that come in decades. (There was a time when monarchs and centuries supplied the temporal unit, but neither count for much anymore.) The 1950s represent an extraordinary time in which postwar affluence, modernism, beats, and the ideology of progress conspired to create a temporal culture that seems vastly more than 40 years away.[98] It now seems another planet — an irony constantly played upon by the space-age bachelor-pad movement.[99] (This irony was there, it turns out, in the original. The great composer of this music genre, Esquivel, called one of his albums "music from a sparkling planet.")

The 1960s are equally strange to us now. Even the people who lived and helped create this decade are estranged from it. The best *Spy Magazine* book on the decade, by Todd Gitlin, a participant, sometimes has a wonderstruck quality about it — as if the author, just a few years later, cannot believe it really happened to him.[100] The 1980s, only a mere handful of years away, also seem most implausible. The great edifice of yuppie self-confidence — with its unapologetic cultivation of hierarchical difference, economic individualism, conspicuous consumption, and competitive self-promotion — is in ruins. Poor Donald Trump, once the "short-fingered vulgarian" so despised by *Spy Magazine*, is no longer emblematic enough to enrage or embarrass. He (and, interestingly, several of his journalistic enemies) no longer matter at all.[101]

We may see plenitude's hand at work here. This is the production of difference—extensive and intensive. Each temporal decade is different and the differences run very deep indeed. Each decade resocializes, supplying new outlooks and aspirations, promoting certain careers and life-goals just as surely as it does certain styles of clothing and music. As it turns out, even *decades* can serve as sunken ships around which new species of social life can establish themselves. And, again, these species are both intensively rich and extensively different.

But temporal cultures are also a way of *managing* difference. They are one of the ways we live with plenitude. We may have, as individuals, committed ourselves to any one (or number of) species by age and gender. We may have, as individuals, committed ourselves to any one (or number of) life-styles. The temporal culture doesn't mind. It is not "particular." It is a little like certain versions of English colonialism or the Roman church, quite prepared to coexist with local loyalties whatever these might be. It says, in effect, whatever else you believe in, believe in me. Whatever else you care about, care about this. Temporal cultures float on the surface of other diversities.

colonialism or the Roman Church

This is handy. Here's diversity that helps us survive diversity. Here is plenitude that forgives plenitude. Here is a way to accomplish commonality even in the face of our present explosive, positively Cambrian, heterogeneity. Every decade we can depend upon a relatively clear and sturdy set of values that establishes a lingua franca, a common code for a collection of increasingly disparate strangers.

So far. But not farther? It is, at this writing, 1997. And eerily quiet. We've been waiting seven years for the decade to declare itself. Naturally, it always takes a few years for this to happen. The 1960s didn't actually start till 1963. The 1970s, of course, never started at all (just kidding). But by 1995 we all began to wonder: "When do we get our marching orders?" When will the decade establish a constellation of values we can navigate by? And we are still waiting. And we will continue to wait. Because it's over. We will not have a decade culture for the 1990s. There's a very good possibility it's just not coming.

Perhaps I'm being hasty. There are several possibilities. One is that these value constellations are really only visible in retrospect. We have to move into the next decade to look back on the old one with any clarity. Tell this to Todd Gitlin who knew exactly what was happening one December evening in 1966 when he heard the anthem of his generation change from *Solidarity Forever* to *Yellow Submarine*.[102] Another possibility is that all of this turns on the approach of the millennium. As long as we are only a few years away from a momentous larger change, why bother with a smaller one? Never mind the decade, let's wait and see what the century holds.

But there is a third and more ominous possibility. And this is that we are now too diverse to have even a "decade culture." Even this lingua franca is perhaps impossible. It may be that nothing will stretch that far. We have those who are still looking for the kinder, gentler decade we were promised at decade's start. We have half the world devoting themselves to simplifying their lives and the other half revelling in a "return to luxury." We have Ani DiFranco and we have Charo. We have people who keep a place in the Hamptons, those who keep a place in AlphaWorld, and those who keep their heads down once the shooting starts. We have those who treat "meat and potatoes" as an article of faith and those for whom it is a Vegan abomination. And this really doesn't begin to inventory the differences of age, gender, life-style, religion, ethnicity, and nationality. Perhaps we're finally beyond consensus. Perhaps we're on the verge of a conflict of Hobbesian proportions. But (contra Hobbes) this will be no war of wills but one of meanings in which every interaction is potentially a collision of cultures.

a place in the Hamptons

WHAT HISTORIANS, ARTISTS, AND FASHION DESIGNERS HAVE IN COMMON

Most historians like things tidy. Most poets couldn't care less. When the editors of a new volume of poetry couldn't find a "common link," that was fine.[103] Poets thrive on chaos. It is where their creativity comes from. Historians are less keen. For them knowledge depends on order. They must sometimes start their work in a welter of possibilities, and, possibly, an archive of heaping confusion. But they must make the data march two by two (and, especially, three by five) towards order and understanding. Plenitude, to the extent it has invaded even the world of knowledge, is especially hard on them. They are tested by what one practitioner calls its "splintering, fragmentation, disarray, shapelessness, inaccessibility, incoherence, chaos, anarchy and meaninglessness." At the end of the day, they want ideas that are "overarching." Less and less frequently do they get them.[104]

We might expect fashion to resemble poetry: to embrace chaos, to thrive on disorder. But no, the world of fashion modelled itself on a monarchical system. Each house was a court, dominated by a prince and ruthless competition with the other great courts.[105] Courts rose and fell, but this was a perfectly hierarchical universe and a place of some clarity. Everyone knew where everyone stood. Not much chaos at all.

In this universe, the new plenitude is a rude, unwelcome, and increasingly frequent guest. When "difference, rather than consensus, [becomes] the order of the day," uneasy lies the crown.[106] It is harder to spot the pretenders, the upstarts, those who would conspire and assemble against the reigning couturier. The prince of fashion once had the advantage of perspective, the ability to command the highest heights. He (till Chanel, always a "he") could spot the enemy from a long way off. Now competitors can come from within, riding a new aesthetic or ethos into fashion. (Yves St. Laurent, meet Claude Montana.) Monarchs also once had the advantage of setting the rules of engagement and controlling the field of battle. This too is more difficult. (Claude Montana, meet *FashionTelevision*.) It is common to remark on the similarities between historians and fashion designers … but here's another commonality: both find the most fundamental rules of discourse challenged by plenitude.

a rude, unwelcome, and increasingly frequent guest

Artists are perhaps more like poets. They don't much care if order is not forthcoming. This makes their disorder easier but not less plentiful. The great "Danto" revelation is well known: in the 1970s artists' definitions of what they did as art changed so much and became so various, it was suddenly impossible to identify a "mainstream" at all. The world of art was now a collection of differences, each artist a kind of tradition unto his or her own. And this made the history of this art, predictably, "all but inscrutable." Plenitude made even the work of the play-by-play announcers impossible.[107]

What is true of history, poetry, fashion, and art is also true of music. Popular music is awash in plenitude. It has always had an exuberant disregard for generic conventions. But it now fizzes with innovation. Punk and heavy metal combined to create, first, grunge and then the (now waning) "alternative" scene. Recently Neil Strauss identified some 22 potential successors.[108] Dance music has thrown off house, ambient, techno, industrial, jungle, trip hop, and illbient.[109] Hip hop has reissued as gangsta, dance hall, trip hop, and acid jazz. We have seen impossible revivals (e.g., surfer, lounge, and ska) and unthinkable combinations (e.g., bagpipe funk from Taxi Chain and swing punk from Big Rude Jake). Diverse elements mix and multiply so routinely that record stores despair of labelling their bins.[110]

Odelay   Widely regarded as the best album of 1996, Beck's *Odelay* is remarkable precisely because it shows so many influences and such diverse ones: folk, rap, rock, blues, funk, country, trip hop, to name a few—all controlled with a fine hand and the ability to manage irony and sincerity, sympathy and ridicule, without the slightest sense of contradiction.[111] This is a hyperplenitude. All the diversity of the world mixing, matching, and multiplying on a single album.

But popular music has always been prepared to change. What are we to make of Yo Yo Ma reaching out of his classical repertoire for Cajun music and Texas fiddle?[112] The classical world defines itself (and the rest of us) by its orthodoxies. Plenitude's cat is amongst the pigeons here and much more must also change.

Even the intellectuals are not immune. The scholars mutter over the "immense fragmentation and privatization of modern literature." They wonder whether this might not "foreshadow ... deeper and more general tendencies in social life as a whole."[113] The very systems by which we manufacture consensus, in Chomsky's phrase, are now challenged by the acknowledgement of differences to which intellectuals contributed so much.[114]

Some intellectuals now complain of a "jumbling" so intense it is no longer possible to classify the world around them. It is too various. It teems so. One of the leading lights of anthropology says with a certain giddy unease, "something is happening to the way we think about the way we think." What he means is, "we are less and less sure how to think at all." For the world, in his words, has become "fluid, plural, uncentered, and ineradicably untidy."[115]

Intellectuals come to this revelation with grave reluctance. (Hence the genius of the Danto revelation.) After all, their job (and some part of their *amour propre*) turns on their agility. Strictly speaking, there should not be any conundrum they cannot parse or penetrate. Good intellectuals like to think of themselves as having Andre Agassi's return of service. There isn't anything to which they can't reply. To admit the world is jumbled, untidy, and beyond the reach of theory is to whimper a little. It is to say that the dragon at the castle's gate may be very much larger and more frightening than anyone reckoned. It is to confess fear and trembling — and the limit of one's competence.

Andre Agassi

What are we to make of the astonishing news that France, the most centrist, rigidly hierarchical nation in the Western world, is now so "fluid" that it is prepared to play host to a "sudden, unexpected diversification?"[116] And what are we to say to the news that America, once the most insular of the Western nations, has given itself over to the "public recognition of national and international differences" as an "essential" element of its culture?[117] Plenitude has found a way not just to vex artists and intellectuals. It is now having its way with nations as well.

There is only one group that appears to have any real comfort with this world. It is the DJ who samples the world for "found sounds" and assembles them into coherent wholes. Tom Rowlands, one half of Chemical Brothers, describes his music this way:

Chemical Brothers

> It's like this puzzle. You spend ages putting things together — things that weren't meant to fit together, disjointed things, things no one would ever think you could put together. And you make something new out of it. It's like magic, sometimes. It's like you're building your own little world.[118]

But when the DJ creates his "own little world," this is perhaps not so much the subjugation of plenitude as its perpetuation. This is *not* order out of disorder. The DJ who would quiet plenitude becomes instead its agent. Indeed, plenitude makes agents of us all. To *live* in plenitude's world means that all of us, artists, intellectuals, DJs, must become the purveyors of plenitude. Certainly, this very book, which would like to be a sober reflection on this new cultural form, is also one more exercise in it — and yet another opportunity for plenitude to extend its hegemony. They also serve who stare in wonder.

Plenitude has been with us always. It was the logic of the first city even as it is the logic of the most recent one.

Aristotle

> The city, Aristotle insists ... is composed of a certain multitude ... but not just any multitude: it must be composed of a multitude that is different in form, eidos, "for the city does not come into being out of those who are similar."[119]

> Utilizing sounds that slide from dub to ambient, jungle to ethnic percussion and found voices to sci-fi soundbites, [illbient] music reflects the mix of past and future, the jumble of cultures and the perpetual salvo of sounds and sights that defines the spectacular intensity of New York City.[120]

Plenitude is also, according to the great man of Western letters, Isaiah Berlin, the very thing that makes us remarkable as a culture.

> It is hardly possible to overrate the value ... of placing human beings in contact with persons dissimilar to themselves, and with modes of thought and action unlike those with which they are familiar.[121]

PLENITUDE SO FAR

Culture by Commotion

- *there are an increasing number of social species*
  e.g., in the place of "standard issue" elderly, there are many kinds of elderly
- *there is depth to each new species*
  e.g., each teen type is intensively different
- *there is difference between these new species*
  e.g., each teen type is extensively different
- *there has been a decisive delinkage of natural and cultural categories*
  e.g., feminism and transgenderism refuse supposed biological foundations of culture
- *cross talk: plenitude provokes plenitude across categories*
  e.g., plenitude among women provokes plenitude among men: feminist revolution helps create new categories of maleness and reaffirm old ones
- *cross talk: plenitude provokes plenitude within categories*
  i.e., plenitude within a community provokes *more* plenitude within that community
  e.g., old species provoke new species within straight, gay, and lesbian communities

- *there can be speciation that marks the end of speciation*
  i.e., some new species resist identifying themselves as such
  e.g., the youngest generation of lesbians refuse a single definition
- *plenitude is opening up and overunning the traditional domains of age and gender*
- *plenitude is opening up and overrunning the domain of life-style*
- *the new species of plenitude are new*
  i.e., they create novel configurations, use old meaning in new ways, and return new meanings to the general culture
- *plenitude may be observed at work in the creation of temporal categories*
  e.g., the decades of this century
- *some kinds of plenitude let us contend with plenitude*
  e.g., temporal cultures establish a kind of lingua franca
- *plenitude appears to be overwhelming even these lingua franca plenitudes*
- *plenitude is infusing history, poetry, fashion, art, music, scholarship, and nationality*
- *plenitude is a mark of urban life and, possibly, a signature of Western culture*

PLATE 12.

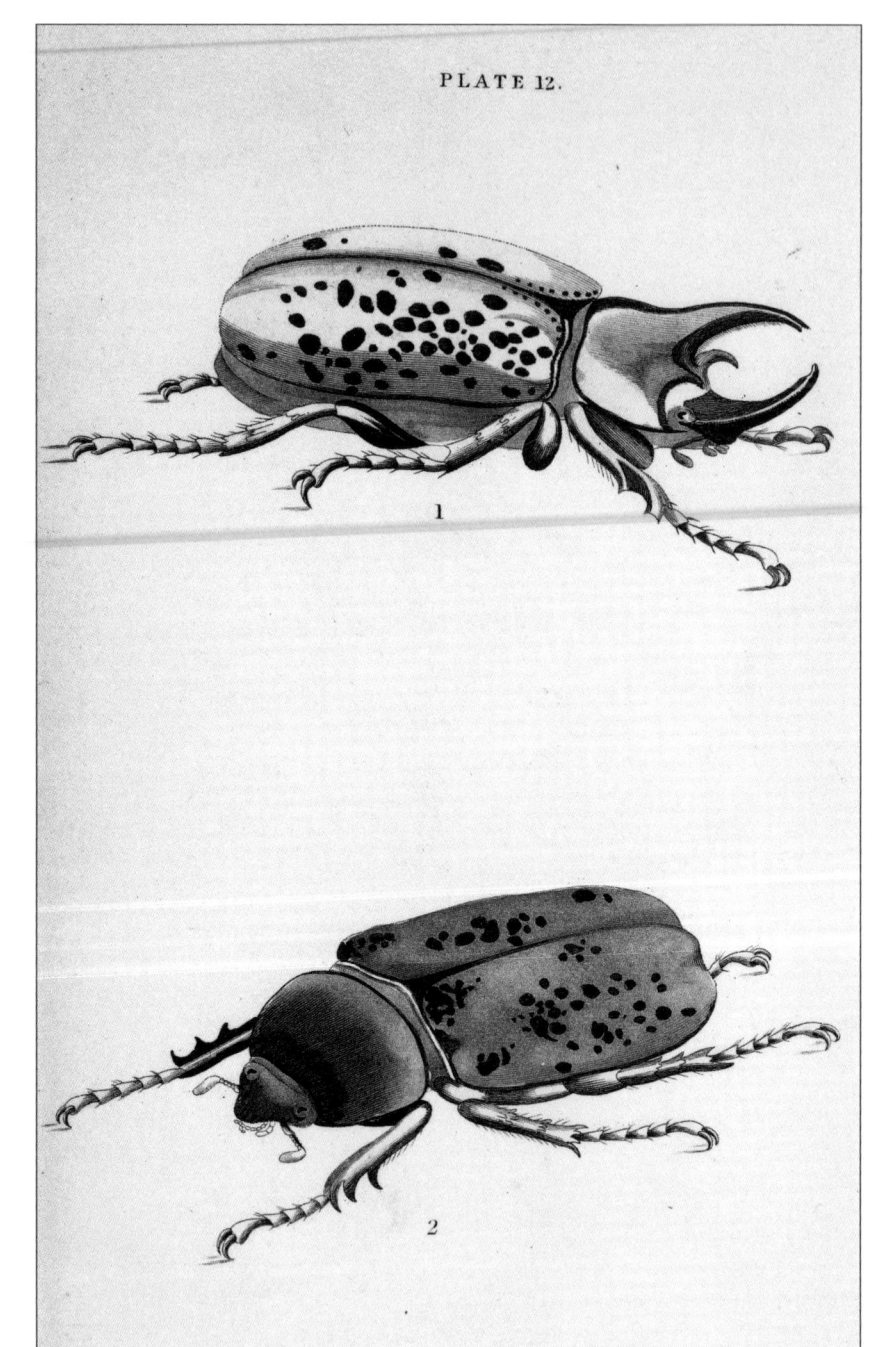

The Withering of the Witherers

INSTITUTIONS

Why should plenitude be flourishing? The explosion of *natural* species that took place in the Cambrian era is sometimes explained according to the "empty barrel" argument.[122] The world played host to so few species there was almost limitless room for their expansion. In an evolutionary version of Parkinson's Law, life expanded to fill the space available to it.

But this should not tempt us as an explanation for social Cambrian explosion. This plenitude appears to come more from the failure of constraints and competitors than from opportunity. Institutions and ideas that once could irradiate new species of social life have been failing. In this section we will look at the decline of the authority of three institutions: family, education, and society; and three ideologies: science, religion, and government. Each of these once acted in the manner of a country club: keeping in the few species, keeping out the many. Each worked in its own way to discourage the production of species and especially the profusion of species. Each now finds that its power to wither is withering.

It's not a good film but it has a good beginning. In *True Lies*, Harry Tasker (played by Arnold Schwarzenegger) exclaims over the fact that his daughter has become a petty thief and wonders how he could ever have failed her so as a parent. Gibb (played by Tom Arnold) laughs and says Tasker mustn't think of himself as her father anymore. Her parents, Gibb explains, are now Madonna and Axel Rose.

Schwarzenegger

In the Reformation scheme of things, families were little commonwealths, dedicated to reproduction of several kinds. One was the inculcation of "godly" values. Every home was charged with the responsibility making "wayward" inclinations and energies run in

49

common channels.[123] Their charge was the production of sameness and the refusal of difference. Families were filters. They were there to reproduce the world.

Axel Rose

Gibb is right. The family is losing this authority and it is doing so because it must compete with people who care nothing for the reproduction of the world. Madonna and Axel Rose are creatures of fashion, fad, and the moment. They are relentlessly promotional of plenitude. Promotional? Madonna and Axel Rose are *agents* of plenitude.[124] They respond to and they reflect new species. Sometimes they are the new species.

Trojan Horse

But plenitude also has a Trojan Horse strategy. It has entered the family and changed it from within.

> [My husband and] I have borne witness to our parents' eight marriages, four divorces, two common-law marriages and one separation. From this bounty, we have collected one "real" sister and seven "real" grandparents, four half-siblings, four stepsisters, four step-parents, two step-grandmothers, two ex-step-parents, two ex-step-grandparents, and one ex-stepbrother.[125]

The stay-at-home-parent family has been joined by the family in which both parents work. The two-parent family has been joined by the single-parent family. (This has come as a special shock because single-parent families used to be something that "only happened in the black community.") The two-parent family has also been joined by the several-parent family (e.g., the family of the six year old who accepts the evidence of her senses and claims four parents.) Marriages designed "for life" are now being joined with ones that presume (or endure) serial monogamy.[126] The pious simplicities of the "nuclear" family have been joined by the complexities of the "blended" family. Different-sex parents are being joined by same-sex parents.

different-sex parents

Everywhere we look, simple, single patterns are giving way to more complex and diverse ones. The nuclear family is no longer the single model or even the majority player. In some communities, children now matter-of-factly ask new acquaintances what kind of family they come from. Heterosexual, one-marriage couples with one or more of their own children are no longer the "safe" assumption.[127]

There is a temptation in certain circles to say new variations are not *models* of the family but merely structural accidents we did not will (and might yet will away). In their wisdom, the U.S. House of Representatives recently passed the Defense of Marriage Act to define marriage as the "union of one man and one woman." But in Western societies, the "accidental" and "unofficial" have a way of becoming structures whether we want them to or not. In any case, there is no reason to suppose the new patterns are going to go away. And the anthropological reality is clear: the children of these "new model" families suffer relatively little confusion or scepticism about these families. As far as they are concerned, their families (one parent, one gender, many splendoured) are structural realities.[128] In the culture of commotion, existing is nine-tenths of the law.

The Protestant family was to be a "cradle" of the larger society, the institutional place where crucial acts of moral development and domestication must take place if they are to occur at all. What happens there has everything to do with what happens elsewhere in the social world. And so, with some irony, it is, in the present case. A newly diverse family helps create a newly diverse society. Children no longer spend their childhoods surrounded by the structural simplicities that used to prevail in prosperous working-class and middle-class communities. They grow up surrounded by many kinds of family and no single kind of home. Second, children must constantly negotiate these complexities in daily life. This shows most plainly in the extraordinary diplomatic skill that some quite young children in North America exhibit. They are accustomed, twice a week, to manage the transition from one household, where certain assumptions prevail, to another, where very different ones do. They have learned to move between these "cultures" with an anthropologist's skill. They have learned a thing or two about diversity. They are living it.

Finally, we have raised our children in the presence of variety and dynamism. Frequently, their families are shifting from one type to another. Melded families keep melding. Who one counts as one's parents, once the simple (and founding) fact of childhood, is now subject to occasional reexamination. New parents come and go. So do siblings. So do in-laws. The contemporary home, Christopher

Lasch's *haven* in a chaotic world, is now a study in dynamism.[129] It is now a cradle that teaches the lessons of fluidity much more than those of fixity.

One illuminating indicator of the change is the way food is prepared and distributed. Not so long ago, the family treated mealtime as a collective event prepared by women and consumed by the family in a ritual event that played out many values and especially patriarchy, the deference of youth to age, and, chiefly, the solidarity of the family unit. We eat together, we *are* together. Since World War II we have seen this pattern change almost beyond recognition. Most families manage only a single "centring" meal a week. The rest of the time food is prepared and consumed episodically. Meals apart is the order of the day. In some families, meals have been replaced by grazing. Without the meal as its ritual centre, the family plays host to less solidarity and more heterogeneity.[130] The family meal is more the exception than the rule — as is the societal form it once promoted.

grazing

All of this says that the family can no longer be the filter it once was. Its ability to remove things from the bloodstream of the body politic has been reduced. What happens "out there" must inevitably happen in the family as well. More to the point, the family has become a place for the production of difference. It is a testing ground for new species. It is now so various, so multiple, so remarkably inconstant in form and structure, that it has passed from removing difference to promoting it.

Education is another institution devoted, traditionally, to the production of sameness. We have always been generous with our talk. Putatively, school was the place the individual could find his or her uniqueness. It was the place selves could work their way skyward towards the warming embrace of a construction-paper sun, each by its own logic, towards its own goals, at its own pace. Thus spake the ideology. The reality was sometimes otherwise. Not infrequently, the affair had a certain hydroponic quality to it.

And there were reasons schools sought sameness. They were educating citizens, with all the high- and entirely single-minded glory that implied. But that wasn't all. Sometimes the school was construed as a kind of backstop. It would catch what the family let slip through. In a perfect world it would refine and perfect the values of the home.

Culture by Commotion

In an imperfect world it would catch the outcome of bad parenting before it became a social problem.

In their time, schools were for good at withering. Kids might go to "sock hops" and have their heads filled with the new music, fast cars, easy sex, turned-up collars, and other Dick Clark–sponsored extravagances. But school was good at bringing them round—at reimposing the authority and the levelheadedness of the adult world.

Nikeworld

Enter Nike, the NBA, and the blindingly charismatic Michael Jordan. These are a siren's call against which the school can find no remotely plausible opposition. Education may control the classroom. Plenitude controls the playground. Education may have the child for several hours every day. But Nikeworld is where they live—in school and out. There is no species Nike does not know about. There is no species Nike can not invent. (Nike mastered social DNA long ago.) And there is almost nothing the school can do about it.

Plenitude washes over schools like hurricanes over the trailer courts of South Florida. Mrs. Johnson, the music teacher, has always been a little clueless—and why should she not. She's a *music* teacher. But now … bless her, she tries hard and, God knows, she means well. Occasionally, she will screw up her courage and ask her students to explain the lyrics of, say, "Stoop" Doggy Dog. There is a roar of laughter. Desks are pounded. Bodies career in all directions. One small mistake and Mrs. Johnson has evoked pet hygiene and leash laws. Lunchtime wits will regale one another with news of that new "stoop and scoop" vibe breaking out of South Central Los Angeles. Everyone will have a good laugh at the expense of Mrs. Johnson and the rest of higher education.

stoop and scoop

Mrs. Johnson is a measure of how little education can wither new species. Snoop Doggy Dog shapes these schoolchildren right down to their magnificent basketball shoes. And it is, I think, fair to say that high school teachers, administrators, and curriculum designers know not a thing about him. One of the reasons the educational system cannot prevent speciation is that it does not begin to understand it.

As usual, plenitude begets plenitude. Parents are sufficiently unhappy with the difficulties of the public system that they are funding an astonishing rise in the number and kind of private schools. This may be taken as a blow against plenitude. Students must wear uniforms and toe the line. But wait! By breaking open the public system from the inside, plenitude creates a new force for diversity on the outside. When parents "vote with their feet" we see a breathtaking speciation of educational philosophy ensue (Montessori, charter, alternative, and religious). Plenitude doesn't care. It isn't particular. How it wins the day matters less than that it does.

Universities might have been the thin red line against the rise of plenitude. A sturdy, uncompromising "canon" might have kept the world at bay.[131] It might have forced a certain meeting of the tribes late in the developmental day. But no. We have seen liberal arts curriculum diminished, disputed, and displaced across the academic world. With the rise of professional programs, fewer students at the undergraduate level are now enrolled in arts programs. Those who are, share no well-defined corpus of classic texts, let alone approach. Many students graduate from liberal arts programs every year without reading, say, Plato, St. Augustine, Descartes, or Mill. Those who do, often would not wish to be asked how these authors created the intellectual and cultural foundations of the Western world, and their culture, and their lives.

Plato, St. Augustine, Descartes, or Mill

The causes of this decline of common ideas are obvious enough. The demands of individual humanities and social sciences (speciating wildly on their own, of course) have chipped away at the liberal arts agenda. Increasingly narrow (read "academically speciated") teachers have lost the ability to address larger issues. Increasingly politicized (read "politically speciated") teachers have happily hijacked liberal arts programs for their own polemical purposes. The famous Tussman experiment at Berkeley, for instance, has repeatedly fallen captive of the ideological enthusiasms.[132] As liberal arts programs have grown more pallid, the demands of the "real world" have grown more feverish. The siren's call of the business program now proves irresistible for some.

The consequences of the decline are equally clear. As long as there is no single body of classic texts, no shared understanding of the undergraduate program, no shared concept of the Western canon, the university surrenders most of its hegemonic powers. It does not stamp each new generation in the image of the elders. It does not domesticate the creative powers of the young in the service of the received wisdom of the old. Each junior generation must be recruited in the name of prevailing values or it can be relied upon to rethink and reinvent these values. Our children will be speciated or speciating. Plainly, they are speciating.

This brings us to the single most important withering of the witherers. There once was a sound. It is produced by pressing the tongue against the top of the mouth, and pulling it back sharply. It produces a kind of "tssszh" sound. This sound once ruled the world. It was the sound of disapproval. It was the way perfect strangers disciplined imperfect strangers. The good matron of society would let fly with one of these when someone boarded the bus unshaven or with their boots unbuttoned. "Tssszh," says the matron. And the imperfect stranger knows he has been tried, judged, and found wanting.

Tssszh was one of the instruments of the status system. There were others: raised eyebrows, middle-distance focal plains, averted gazes, sour faces. (Any good maitre d' remains a study in all these techniques.) And the instruments are all now mostly dead. I hear "tssszh" from time to time on public transit. A Toronto matron will draw herself up to her full height and dignity — and let fly. The offender will look at her with curiosity and in many cases absolutely no comprehension. Those who do comprehend, wonder what the matter is. Most who do know what the matter is, do not care. At all. No one is, forgive me, cowed. The sound is now just a sound (listen also for grinding metaphors) — the call of the Toronto matron. For it no longer signifies anything of social import. It is of ornithological interest only. The matron is now just one species among many.

any good maitre d'

This marks the decline of a status system, a notion of hierarchy, that was once the great single, almost exclusive speciator of Western societies. It took the great and sprawling masses of these societies and arranged them into a vertical set of classes, insisting on the right of higher parties to disapprove (tssszh!) of lesser parties and the obligation of lesser parties to emulate higher ones.[133] This is probably the single most important *social* idea in the Western tradition. (Sir Thomas Elyot writing in the 16th century is firm on this point: "...it may not be *called* ordre [order], excepte it do contayne in it degrees, high and base...."[134]) More to our present purpose, it could, in its time, claim to be the most important speciator in Western society and the one that discouraged virtually all others.[135]

slaves One of the great strengths of this system is that it allowed for people to change but drove them all in the same direction. When Frances Trollope came to visit America in the 1820s, she was not so distracted by her flight from English bankruptcy that she failed to notice the manners of people around her.

> The lady I now visited ... greatly surpassed my quondam friends in the refinement of her conversation. She ambled through the whole time the visit lasted, in a sort of elegantly mincing familiar style of gossip, which, I think, she was imitating from some novel, for I was told she was a great novel reader, and left all household occupations to be performed by her slaves.[136]

Trollope's discovery was not an exceptional one. Novels were, for many, life-style instructions. They helped individuals of one class glimpse, and so imitate, the manners of another, higher, one.[137] Thus were species identified and subscribed to. Thus were creative energies commandeered.

When people thought to change themselves, when they sought out new ideas and behaviours, they looked to the species above them for their inspiration. "Status emulation," as this is sometimes called, was the great template for transformation in 19th century society. It is how people changed. It is why they changed. "Comme il faut" controlled many thoughts and actions. The phrases "one must" and "one mustn't" ruled most public (and many private) performances of the self.[138] With their energies thus directed and absorbed, there wasn't much likelihood that individuals would undertake the invention of other species of social life.

How completely the status system claimed and absorbed creative energies may be observed from the Western obsession with two rooms in the home (for those lucky enough to have them): the living room and the dining room. The size, furnishings, condition, and "tone" of these rooms were, typically, the best, most self-aggrandizing status statement the individual could muster. For the dining room, plate and silver were key measures of wealth and standing. It was by these rooms the householder would be judged. (This is, for instance, why living rooms were—and are—separated off and kept inviolate with velvet ropes and, sometimes, plastic coverings—to keep the status statement pristine.) The status system was so powerful in its control of emotional and economic resources it could force even this ceremonial "destruction" of wealth. And with control of this order, transgressive alternatives were unthinkable.

Well, there was one transgression that did occur. It was not uncommon for Westerners to engage in a little creative licence when they fashioned their status statements. Occasionally, they would "bump up" their speech, clothing, mannerisms to make themselves a little grander than was, strictly speaking, warranted. In the worst cases, they invented ancestors, buying up the portraits of perfect strangers and claiming them as kin. They wore school ties they were not entitled to. They engaged in status counterfeiting of several kinds.[139]

But, astonishment of astonishments, even when individuals were *disobeying* the status system, they remained its captives. All their "transgressive" energy and inclination was commandeered. Nothing remained for other speciating purposes. Hierarchy and status won even when abused. They prevailed even when they appeared to fail.

disobeying the status system

The status system lives on in some corners of our society, and plainly it enjoyed a vigorous renaissance in the 1980s.[140] But overall it has diminished in influence. We have seen a levelling influence, devaluing and displacing experts and elites everywhere. True, we still have Martha Stewarts who would inform us of the best and most effective construction of our status statements. But listen to one of her rivals and another arbiter of the status code:

> What I hope to do is allow people to feel freer about setting tables. … You needn't be worried about mixing your grandmother's china with Pottery Barn and antiques. If you don't have matching pieces and bought some plates at the flea market, it doesn't matter.[141]

The terrible scrutiny to which every individual, and especially female head of household, was subject has let up a little. There is no longer a place of final reckoning within the home that must be preserved at great expense and with great anxiety. Indeed, there is no moment of final reckoning, no visit from the pastor, or a high-ranking neighbour, to defend oneself against. But most important, less and less is there a *standard* of final reckoning. Hierarchy still counts for something in our lives, but so many other grounds and measures of speciation exist that it is now merely one voice among many.

Pandora's box

Over the course of the present century we have watched hierarchy steadily decline, opening a Pandora's box of possibilities. Now unexpected and implausible groups can have their influence. Children from the streets of Liverpool or Manchester invent punk. Gay men change the clothing styles of straight men. Gangs from South Central Los Angeles invent hip hop. Lesbians change the hairstyles of straight women. Garage bands from Seattle invent an alternative sound. The Black Panthers, in their day, find a place in the drawing rooms of Manhattan's Upper East Side. Now influence "trickles up" from the "bottom" of society.[142] Matrons may tssszh but it matters less and less.

Black Panthers

It is hard to reckon with the sheer scale of this development. After all, hierarchy has traditionally been the Western way of dealing with plenitude. It was the Aristotelian solution to the Platonic problem. The way to order and bind up the endless diversity of the world, said Aristotle, was to establish a continuum of status. Rank things high and low, and the diversity takes on system, order, proportion. We are on the verge of dispensing with hierarchy as the great "operator" in the Western tradition.[143] It is not clear what we have in its place. More exactly, without the withering power of the status system, we have many things in its place.

The decline of hierarchy complicates the social world enormously. Hierarchy had extraordinary classificatory power. It could be used to assess any person, object, or event. It was the perfect all-purpose social compass. It supplied everything from the seating arrangements at a state banquet to the best tie to wear to work. In its place, there are many competitors: naturalism, authenticity, competitiveness, homeyness, irony. It is not clear that any has the incisive or encompassing evaluative power of hierarchy. And it is unlikely that any will rise to a position of preeminence. We live in a world of many, conflicting, evaluative schemes, a world where every social assessment comes equipped with its own contradiction.

The forces for plenitude appear in every direction. It is not just trickle up but trickle in. Wrestling, tattooing, tractor pulls, tabloid journalism, and weight lifting used to live on the margins of polite society. As long as middle-class morality was governed by upper-class *tractor pulls* tastes, this is where they stayed, devalued as vulgar and off limits. Now that hierarchy has lost its hegemony, these can flourish and they do. Country and western music has moved from the despised hinterland of our society into its very centre. In roughly six years, country and western star Garth Brooks sold some seven million records.[144]

The causes of hierarchy's decline are many. The 1960s and 1970s, with revolutions in music, self-presentation, sexuality, and politics, made a signal contribution. At the very least, they gave egalitarian ideas new currency.[145] But longer-term developments had their effect as well. Hollywood has replaced high society as our great exemplar.[146] High-status families struggle without success to master the complexities of the contemporary world and often fail to be exemplary (e.g., England's royal family). The upper echelon now consists of competing elites (e.g., art, science, media, business, society) instead of a single one. Higher ups have pursued fashion when their hegemony depended upon the cultivation of a code of their own.[147]

As a society, we care less about sincerity of role and more about authenticity of self.[148] Hierarchy interests less, constrains less, inspires less. We are no longer gratified by note-perfect performances or the dumb show of good manners. We now prefer the cultivation of essential, emergent selves in a noisier, more various social world. There is no authoritative tssszh to tell us otherwise.

IDEOLOGIES

We have seen the decline of several ideas that once possessed great withering powers. When these ideas were robust, most novel species of social life were simply impossible. They might emerge here or there. But they could not survive for long in the "nuclear winter" imposed by these ideologies. Those that did survive could only do so on the far margins of social life: basement coffeehouses, bars in the "wrong part of town," seaside, carnival, or tourist towns where standards were known to be "lax." There were three of these ideologies in particular: science, religion, and government.

In the postwar period, science was a privileged form of discourse. It was the most credible "way of knowing" at our disposal. It was the great linchpin between progress on one side and technology on the other. It was the way progress was accomplished; it was the great fund of knowledge on which technology drew. It was a shrine of national aspiration, and North Americans deferred before it. Science was asked to specify the best arrangements for domestic living (medicine and home economics), the best way of organizing the world of work (time and motion studies), the best way of intervening with nature (hydroelectric projects), and the best way to address social problems (e.g., Kennedy's Camelot project). It was regarded as the final authority on many topics.[149]

eggheads

There were two groups of high priests in the shrine of science. One was, of course, scientists. These were often depicted as unworldly eggheads, much too smart actually to be good for anything of worldly significance. The other group were doctors, and, astonishingly, North America made these men and women arbiters of almost every aspect of social life. It made perfect sense that they be consulted for advice on what to do about the common cold. But they were also consulted on when driving licences might be obtained for

suburbia

particular teens, and what should be done for housewives driven more or less mad by life in 1950s suburbia. They were our village wise men, despite the fact that, in many ways, their training took them away from, not towards, the wisdom they were being asked to "dispense."

Scientific authority was seen to be so powerful and thoroughgoing that there was virtually no aspect of personal and social life for which it would not be useful. It is not too much to say that scientific authority was the arbiter of this personal and public life. And in this capacity it was an extraordinarily powerful withering agent. Medical authority was almost deeply conservative authority. It was positively papal in its orthodoxy and monarchical in its self-assurance.

Today the authority of science is in some question. The causes here are numerous. The egalitarian shift has made us less awestruck by the status of scientists and doctors. The rise of naturalism has made science look, sometimes, like runaway artifice — when it is not actually being construed as an act of sexual aggression against mother earth. Science's once vaunted powers of mastery and control of nature are now widely seen as the cause of our environmental degradation. The compounds and chemicals once heralded as "progress in a pill" are now the creations of reckless, arrogant, greedy men in lab coats. Next to big business, scientists are the villains of the piece.

Doctors have taken it especially hard. The exemplar here was Dr. Welby (can that really have been his name?), a man of great sensitivity and unashamed patriarchal stature. Increasingly Americans see doctors as rather more self-interested, rather less Hippocratic. But there are deeper, symptomatic changes. Illness is no longer "malfunction." The body is now a complicated web of energies, forces, and powers previously unguessed. The patient now demands to be treated as a "whole person." Some part of the medical community responds to these cultural changes. Some much larger part exercises an Olympian disdain and makes the whole thing a good deal worse.

Dr. Welby

As a result, science and medicine have lost some of their power as social arbiters and their ability to wither the new. Now the oak has fallen, a hundred flowers bloom. We are now prepared to believe in a great many things for which there is no good scientific warrant. This includes everything from minor cold remedies like Echinacea (a cold remedy that derives from the Black Sampson root) to the healing powers of the cult of Elvis.[150] Even deeply conventional people routinely ionize air and purify tap water — often without clear scientific justification. (I know a dentist who has buried crystals in his yard to "balance the harmonics of the house.") Virtually everyone is prepared to believe things that just 15 years ago we would have insisted upon taking before the court of science before embracing.[151]

Science was an arbiter of basic questions of identity. No longer. Gordene Olga MacKenzie argues for the term "transgenderist" *precisely* "because it is not medically applied but 'self generated.'"[152] Twenty years ago, no individual could have successfully defied the medical community in this way and invented their own diagnostic category. They would have been denied an audience and a publisher.

But now that science no longer plays "traffic cop," refusing some ideas and certifying others, a world of novelty blooms. This arbiter of gender, family life, and human nature has been eclipsed and left us with a vastly larger imaginative envelope of possibilities.

The authority of organized religion has been challenged as well. There was a time when people gathered each week for a recalibration of the moral compass and to be reminded of the "first principles" of daily existence. As church attendance falls and as religious scepticism rises, the persuasive power of the church shapes us less and less. As one scholar puts it, there has been a "breakdown of the religio-cultural consensus that was once assumed to prevail in Christianized societies of the West."[153] (I defer for later treatment the rise of the religious Right.)

Out from under the shadow of the great cathedrals, a hundred flowers bloom here too. We are now prepared to seek the counsel of iridologists, psychics, yogis, witches, gurus, shamans, astrologers, and the child within.[154]

From a self-proclaimed shaman called Thunderhorse, who roams the Southwest with a few disciples, to followers of Rael, a 51-year-old former race-car driver from France who believes humans were created in laboratories by aliens, [cults] spread their messages and seek converts. "It's not a question of what's out there, but what isn't out there," says Janja Lalich of Alameda, Calif., a 52-year-old cult expert.[155]

The irony is strong. People who find themselves unable to suspend disbelief in a conventional church or synagogue suffer no such difficulty in an unconventional one. Having thrown off organized religion as implausible, they are now prepared to embrace any number of alternative spiritual schemes, however implausible they might seem.[156] I do not mean to mock this new credulity, but merely to point out how generous is the environment it creates for new beliefs. There is a new credulity at large in the land. It welcomes cultural inventions of virtually every kind.[157] It withers nothing.

Government has lost credibility and authority as well. Citizens are now prepared to entertain accounts of contemporary events that depart in every particular from the "official" version. Citizens are prepared to accept that the U.S. government has systematically covered up evidence of interplanetary visitation, for instance. The vastly popular television program *The X-Files* turns almost entirely upon this theme. (And its numbers are perhaps some reckoning of the scale of our scepticism. *The X-Files* has 30 million viewers and 100 Net sites.[158]) Citizens will attend the Conspiracy Museum in Dallas, devoted to the assassination of John F. Kennedy, and listen without astonishment when they are told, "You must never forget, the Warren Report is a lie." One museum visitor expressed some discomfort with this bald assertion but concluded, "There is one thing for sure, ... it didn't happen like [the government] said it happened."[159]

evidence of interplanetary visitation

Credulity finds its way everywhere. But it is not unusual to hear well-educated, otherwise sophisticated individuals contend that General Electric long ago invented the eternal electric light bulb and that General Motors invented a car that runs on matchbook covers.

Consider this experiment, if you will. Here is a *fictitious* scenario:

> The scientists in Utah *did* invent cold fusion but the interests of business, governments, and the scientific establishment were so threatened the scholars were forced to fake experimental failure and bury the formula. They were bought off. Follow the money.

The present intellectual climate is so richly oxygenated with scepticism that virtually any contention may appear plausible. Or, better, we are in our scepticism so little sceptical, we are prepared to believe anything. Even this.[160]

In such a climate many species are plausible. Or, more exactly, in such a climate almost no species is implausible. When the authority of government is compromised, every act of imagination, every conspiracy theory, becomes a little more robust. When the authorities of science, religion, and government together are compromised, the world simply explodes. Virtually anything is now possible. In the Platonic formula with which we opened the book: Whatever can be imagined will someday be. ✺

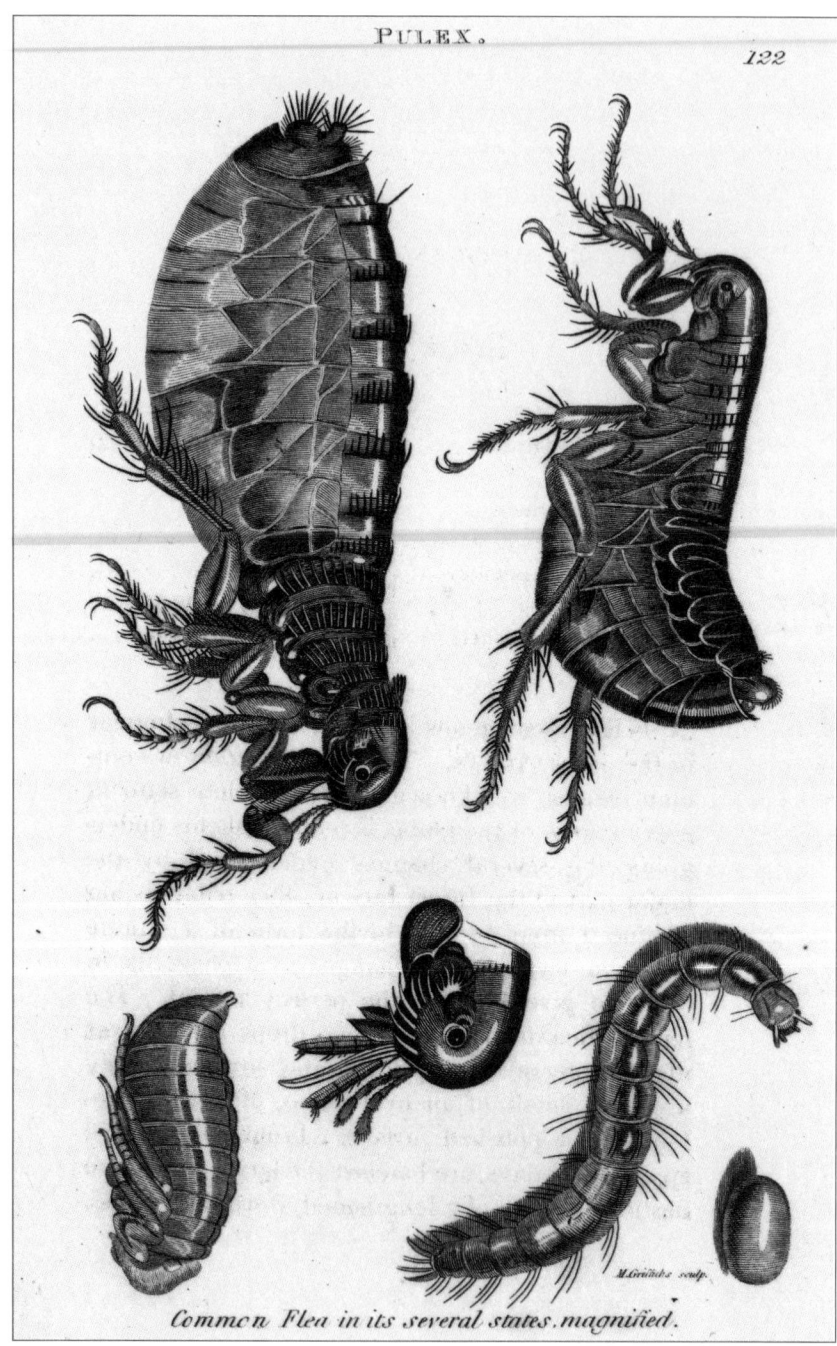

M.Griffith sculp.

Common Flea in its several states, magnified.

Withering Still

WORK

The world of work remains the great bulwark of conformity, a great enemy of the production of difference. Those who work for the corporation frequently find their lives constrained by it. There was once such a thing as the "company man," a creature who lived in a very narrow envelope. Joining some companies was very like joining the military. There were clear rules. There was a demanding "corporate culture," according to which the individual was obliged to conform, both on and off the job. The corporate culture could dictate how one lived, where one lived, how one voted, and even (unofficially) who one married.[161]

Most irksome, the corporation could even commandeer the emotional life of the worker, obliging airline hostesses and sales people to counterfeit emotions for the sake of sales. To the extent that our culture treats the emotional domain as a private one, this has been taken as a measure of how the corporation could control and constitute the individual, how much it could interfere with the essentials of selfhood.[162]

Daniel Bell, in his relentlessly brilliant *Cultural Contradictions of Capitalism*, lets us see that the corporate control of selfhood represents a conflict between economic individualism and expressive individualism.[163] The first individualism demands an *instrumental* self dedicated to "getting the job done" and prepared to subordinate all claims of individuality to this objective. But expressive individualism says we must express our creativity and differences.

This conflict between economic and expressive individualisms is a founding contradiction of Western societies. It is unlikely that one of these individualisms will eclipse the other, but it does appear that expressive individualism enjoys the upper hand. (And when expressive individualism wins, so does plenitude.) It has been advanced by the recent *reengineering* of the corporation. This was, among other things, an attack on the instrumental, corporate man, forcing him out in favour of those who can live more fully by their wits. Irony of ironies, in some corporate circumstances the only way to fulfil economic individualism is through expressive individualism. Business is becoming more *ad hoc*, a matter of spontaneous and creative problem solving that must be left increasingly to the individual's devices. Sometimes, the men and the women of the corporation are more the authors of the corporation than the other way around.[164]

In the realm of small business, expressive individualism (and plenitude) has won several *de facto* victories. Generation Xers have been obliged to take up "McJobs," or to piece careers together out of a job here and a job there.[165] In this event it is more difficult for the workplace to make overweening demands. The individual is freed (and forced) to invent themselves for their own purposes by dint of their own activities. The corporation has less (or no) coercive power.

The long-term prospect is not clear. In some sectors for some jobs, instrumental individualism continues to press down hard. To this extent, the individual is obliged to adopt a relatively prefab self and to live the life of the "corporate man." In these cases (and these cases continue to characterize the working lives of many millions of Westerners), plenitude is suppressed. More exactly, work works to wither the possibility of new species of social life and self-expression. Sometimes less oppressive rules apply and plenitude may be expected to flourish. I will not venture a guess as to where the long-term trend will take us. It is enough to say two things. First, that the withering power of work continues to work against the invention and expression of plenitude. And, second, these withering powers are, in some places, under challenge.

A word on the scourge of franchising. Franchising has helped erase local, regional, and individual differences and impose a national sameness. It has played the friend of uniformity and the enemy of plenitude. Thus, for instance, the unpredictable inclinations of the local hotdog stand ("Larry's! Good! Eats!") have been increasingly replaced by numbing pleasantries devised by some not very imaginative home office. This is nowhere more obvious or more offensive than in the strip mall or the fast-food alley. Franchising design is informed chiefly by the fear of giving offence. It is inclined to make the world slippery with false bonhomie. It erases eccentricity, individuality, and difference. It creates a world that has, in Gertrude Stein's famous words, "no there there."

There is some movement here. McDonald's outlets no longer all look alike. But it is probably still true that home office approves all variation and departure. Does home office understand the implications of living in the world that plenitude has built? Where once the most important product was the guarantee of sameness and uniformity, what "sells" increasingly is variation (at least in design). All of the "waterfront" and "downtown" renovations of the last 10 years have made this plain. The rise of the local (micro) brewery makes this plain. The decline of the department store and the rise of the boutique make this plain. Everywhere we look we see the great institutions and inclinations of uniformity giving way to the play of variation and heterogeneity. But it is impossible to know how far the corporate world will let this go. Here, as above, we live in a moment when uniformity and diversity are locked in a struggle the outcome of which cannot be predicted. The witherer continues to wither — even as it appears, in places, to be giving way.

SPORTS

Another institution that has worked to wither new species and the blossoming of plenitude is sport. Every child raised by Madonna and Axel Rose comes into contact with a coach who is much less solicitous of difference and rather more demanding of sameness. Sports demands discipline, uniformity, and subordination of self to team, and to this extent team membership can be powerfully withering of social speciation. Or to put this another way, when Mrs. Johnson is a music teacher she has relatively little power to fight off the pressure that popular culture creates on behalf of plenitude. But when she is the volleyball coach, things change dramatically. *This* Mrs. Johnson can reach into the lives of her teenage wards and exact extraordinary

acts of conformity. This Mrs. Johnson can fight plenitude and sometimes win.

Like work, sport has been an increasingly important bulwark
against plenitude. As other institutions and ideologies fall away, it
begins to assume more and more importance. It is rather as if the
child's experience of the world is mostly shaped by Bell's "expressive
individualism" and, in childhood, it is sometimes only the world of
sport in which he or she will be introduced to his "instrumental individualism." This is another way of saying that in the world of the
child virtually everything points in the direction of plenitude with the
exception of the socialization that takes place in the domain of sport.
By this reckoning there are then two domains in the culture of commotion that resist the blandishments and imperatives of plenitude:
sports in childhood and work in the teen and adult years.

But if expressive individualism has made inroads in the world of
work, it has certainly also done so in the world of sport. There was a
time when the individual and anything like individual innovation was
slam dunk   submerged within the team. No body politic was ever more demanding of conformity and the effacement of the individual. But we have
seen this change. Uniforms that were once entirely uniform have
given way to the individuation, first, of numbers and, then, names.
Notre Dame and Penn State are perhaps the last college football programs to resist this trend. Tattoos on basketball players and "styling"
on the part of football players have also helped to break through the
"uniformity" of sport. Trash talking and spectacular gestures during
a slam dunk in basketball or when entering the end zone in football
have become "signatures" for the individual athlete. Michael Jordan
is fully individuated on and off the court and subsumed by nothing,
not his team, not the sport, not his race, not even his celebrity.[166] (I
think one could argue that basketball has come out of relative obscurity and disrepute to rival sports like baseball, football, and hockey
precisely because players are less concealed by a laconic tradition in
the sport or all the protective equipment which so obscures facial
expression and emotion. In basketball, you could finally *see* the person in the player/team/sport.)

But for most kids in most sports for most purposes, participation
has a chilling effect. It remains a great witherer of what might other-

wise be their transgressive energies and certainly their innovative ones. Watching sport may have this effect as well—especially when sport serves as a "gender pageant." Like work, sports shows the influence of plenitude and leans more and more in an "expressive" direction. But it is also true to say that this witherer withers still.

MARKETING

The era of mass marketing is still upon us. According to this model, all creative ideas are measured against their ability to maximize sales. This turns some business deliberations into an exercise in the obvious. And things turn especially nasty when creative teams are "brought to heel" by the marketing team. Here is filmmaker Cameron Crowe (*Fast Times at Ridgemont High*, 1982; *Singles*, 1992; *Jerry Maguire*, 1996) on how it works in Hollywood:

> You have more and more people coming into the tent with the creative guys. You have marketing and concept testers, advertising people. What you find gets the high numbers is easily appealing subjects: a baby, a big, broad joke, a high concept. Everything is tested. The effect is to lessen the gamble, but in fact you destroy a writer's confidence and creativity once so many people are invited into the tent.[167]

More disturbingly, perhaps, marketing directs the publisher's hand as well. As Mark Crispin Miller points out, books are increasingly written for market, instead of being written and taken to market.[168] Sometimes this works on the behalf of plenitude, for it forces the publisher to speak to readers' interests and not his or her notion of what these interests are (or ought to be). But when the effect of marketing calculations is to force a "regression towards the mean" in so far as publishers will risk nothing that does not promise "big numbers," then something quite different is happening. Now marketing prevents the possibility that emergent, and usually small, species of social life can find a place beneath the publisher's sun. Add to this the concentrations of ownership and a certain disinclination to self-criticism that Miller also notes, and the world of book publishing looks less and less like a potential nursery of difference.

Cultural institutions of every kind (museums, operas, symphonies, theatres) now feel the pressure to speak to a broader public. Often the marketing "function" within them is elevated accordingly. There can be moments when this function contributes to a "dumbing down" of the institution in question. Marketing may, for instance, encourage yet another production of *The Nutcracker Suite* when plenitude would be much better served by a different, more difficult production. But, again, there are other moments when marketing plays a democratizing role, opening up topics and treatments that these elitist institutions would otherwise disdain.[169]

dark rumours

Marketing's hand can even be seen where it, apparently, has no place. The alternative movement in popular culture was created expressly to encourage music and film unsullied by the marketing influence. But dark rumours swirl. It is suggested that one of the most popular of the alternative artists (an evident contradiction in terms), Alanis Morissette, was a creation by the marketing team associated with Madonna's recording studio, that she was invented to capture "market share." We need to acknowledge how this blunts the full creative potential of a society devoted to plenitude (even as we acknowledge how thoroughgoing was Morissette's contribution to the spread of the alternative "species" as an addition to our plentiude).

Plainly there is a movement away from mass marketing, especially as the entertainment and cultural industries are forced to respond to the heterogeneity of the world before them. As we will see in a section to come ("Plenitude's Fellow Travellers"), marketing can be an agent of diversity as well. The trick, in a society constructed by plenitude, is to acknowledge both inclinations. It is clear, for instance, that both are at work in the new "bifurcated" structure of the recording and movie industries. Large studios and labels continue to dominate the landscape and turn out mainstream titles for a mass audience. We also see an increasing number of "independents," some of whom are owned by the large studios and labels. Certainly, these independents are marketing-driven creatures. They give the big studio/label "street" credibility, the ability to recruit new artists and track new trends. But they also give the big studio/label new versatility and adaptability as well as the opportunity to address, and create, heterogeneity and difference.

Some argue marketing once ruled the consumer culture, that plenitude was kept at bay (and contained) by its withering power.[170] This proposition was once certainly true, but it is now quite wrong. Corporations now have no choice but to respond to our new diversity. Anything else is a recipe for obscurity. So even marketing is now being colonized by plenitude. It may still wither but not for long. And when it is fully colonized by plenitude, the sky, as they say, is the limit.

THE DISNEY™ DANGER

Copyright and corporate control can be powerfully withering. The force of law, the protection of property, the exercise of proprietary control swim like sharks through the world of plenitude, consuming innovation here, refusing borrowing there. The corporation guards its lair.

Sometimes of course the relationship between the corporation and the new species works to the advantage of the corporation. It is hard to imagine hip hop culture without the logos and products from the NBA, Nike, Sprite, to name just three. Boots from Doc Marten's *Hell's Angels* were seized upon by punks, skinheads, hard-core, and alternative cultures. The Hell's Angels and Harley Davidson motorcycles are inseparable. Jeans from Levi-Strauss became "species wear" for virtually everyone caught up in the revolts of the 60s and beyond. Lacoste shirts were a key symbol for the early preppie movement as Ralph Lauren was for the later one. In sum, corporations are sometimes embraced as the emblems of new social species, and the relationship works to their profit.

But there are moments when plenitude and the corporation collide. This has been especially evident in the *sampling* movement that has emerged in the last few years. In this case, the copyrighted property of the corporation is pressed into service — recycled as it were —

in new creative undertakings. Thus we hear a phrase from *Out of Sight* by James Brown on Beck's *Odelay*. Hundreds of bits and pieces of "corporate property" are being "appropriated" by artists in this way, and, to judge by appearances, the corporations are not happy about it.

As we move into a *sampling* culture, this issue will grow steadily more problematical. In a sampling culture, old cultural elements live on in the new. We have seen this inclination in the world of art since the appearance of the "readymades" of Marcel Duchamp. We have seen it in music since the appearance of John Cage right through to the "found sound" tradition that Jason Fine tells us is now poised to take over popular music.[171] We have seen it in TV shows like *The Simpsons* which quotes, references, and recycles the stuff of popular culture. We have seen it in comedy routines everywhere, with Dennis Miller being the most self-conscious example.[172]

A sampling culture is a natural development in the world of plenitude. The "turnaround time" is reduced. No need to let things "mulch" very much. No sooner has something appeared in one form than it may be pressed into service in another. The artist/innovator hardly needs to remove the packaging, as it were. Things are taken whole—and combined without much ceremony (though in the best cases with real cunning). In a sampling culture, one piece of our disparate culture is struck sharply against another that novelty might insue. Sampling and plenitude work well together.

The sampling tradition strikes terror into the hearts of the corporation. From the copyright holder's point of view, sampling is larceny. As Misha Glouberman has demonstrated, the issue is particularly acute on the Web where the "appropriation" of graphics, logos, music, or even themes is met with a brisk and often hostile legal reply.[173] Toys-R-Us, for instance, went after Roadkills-R-Us on the grounds that their name might some how be tarnished.[174] This is ludicrous but not uncommon.[175]

Aaron Spelling (producer of *Love Boat, Fantasy Island, Charlie's Angels*) is responsible for some of the worst television of our time (in the way that the Catholic church is, as Tom Wolfe once pointed out, responsible for a good deal of our kitsch). But his lawyers are aggressively challenging a Web page devoted to *Melrose Place*. One would think that a man like Spelling might encourage the appropriation and reworking of his work. There's always the possibility that someone might redeem it with intelligent treatment.[176]

But here is an irony worth reckoning with. The owners of *The Simpsons* copyright are being extremely aggressive in their pursuit of Web pages that feature materials from this show. This despite the fact that the show has helped itself to hundreds of themes, idioms, tag lines, characters, and character types produced by commercial culture in the last 10 years. I quote a recent letter from Fox lawyers to a *Simpsons* Web page owner in full:

It has come to our attention that you have caused the creation and distribution of a collection of icons which reproduce the characters, images, voices, sounds and other distinctive elements of the copyrighted television series entitled, "THE SIMPSONS". Twentieth Century Fox Film Corporation ("Fox") owns all rights under copyright and trademark in and to "THE SIMPSONS". Your creation and distribution of these icons patently and unavoidably infringes Fox's rights.

This course of conduct exposes you to substantial monetary damages and injunctive relief in favor of Fox. As you may be aware, such damages for copyright infringement can include statutory penalties of as much as $100,000 for willful infringement, damages under laws governing trademarks, and punitive damages under laws of unfair competition.

In view of the foregoing, we hearby demand that you do the following:

1. Immediately cease and desist all further creation, distribution, advertising, promotion, posting or any other exploitation of the referenced icons, or any other activity which utilizes the characters, images, voices, sounds, designs or other elements of "THE SIMPSONS" in any way whatsoever;

2. Immediately order all such icons, as well as all related artwork, and other materials, or any other use thereof, to be withdrawn;

3. Deliver to a designated representative of our office all disks containing such icons, all related artwork, or any other materials on hand;

4. Provide Fox with an itemized accounting of any and all revenues resulting from exploitation of such icons so that Fox can determine its damages;

5. Provide Fox with the names and addresses of all persons to whom such infringing icons have been sold and/or distributed, or who are known to you to have received, used and/or further distributed such icons. In addition, please provide Fox with the names of all internet servers on which you know such icons have been posted.

6. Confirm to the undersigned in writing, by letter received in our office not later than 5:00 p.m. on November 10, 1995, that you shall fully and promptly comply with each of the foregoing demands (at which time specific arrangements for turnover of materials can be finalized).

If we have not received your full and voluntary compliance with each of the foregoing demands by the deadline specified, be advised that we shall, without further notice to you, take all available legal action to compel the discontinuation of your use and exploitation of the infringing icons, to recover monetary damages to the full extent allowed by law, including attorney's fees and costs of suit, and to obtain such additional legal and/or equitable relief as the court may allow in the circumstances. We hope that your voluntary compliance with the foregoing reasonable and lawful demands will make the initiation of legal action against you unnecessary.

Finally, be advised that nothing contained in this letter is intended as, or may be deemed or construed to constitute, a waiver or relinquishment of any of Fox's rights and remedies in the premise, all of which are hereby expressly reserved.[177]

It is really too strange that this letter should come from a *Simpsons* lawyer. In a just world, Evil Knievel, Leonard Nimoy, Dustin Hoffman, George and Barbara Bush, Linda and Paul McCartney, Arnold Schwarzenegger, and everyone else whose persona has been appropriated for *The Simpsons* would reply in kind, slap a cease and desist order on them, and that would be the end of it. Why should Fox have it both ways? Surely Matt Groening, possibly the wittiest man in America, can see the absurdity of this situation.

the
wittiest man
in America

Certainly there are good grounds for copyright anxiety. Here are three:

- The offending party fails to frame the appropriation so that it can be seen *as* an appropriation. In this case, the viewer doesn't know they are *not* looking at a Fox rendition of *The Simpsons*, and, therefore, cannot tell that they are looking at someone else's rendition.
- The offending party profits directly and substantially from the appropriation. In this case, the consumer must buy the record/image/magazine especially to acquire the copyrighted material. This condition cannot apply when the copyrighted material is a minor part of the record/image/magazine in question. A flicker of James Brown on Beck's *Odelay* does not qualify.
- The offending party inflicts permanent damage upon the character or content of the copyrighted material. In this case, the reworking of an image of Homer Simpson would have to change substantially the way the viewer thinks about this image. It should be noted how rarely this happens and usually only as the result of astonishingly good satire. I, for one, can think of only one recent instance in which it has occurred. The Canadian radio program *Double Exposure* portrayed a cabinet minister as Robert DeNiro in the "you lookin' at me" scene from *Taxi Driver*. The satire was so effective, so devastating, that many Canadians could never think of the minister the same way again. Her public persona was effectively destroyed. The Canadian airwaves are filled with satirical materials — hundreds of hours each year. That this, for one viewer, should be the *only* time the satirical object was substantially changed is some indication of how rarely this condition applies.

Homer Simpson

There are also very good grounds for caution. If the world of plenitude *is* becoming a sampling culture, we should expect the rules of intellectual property to change accordingly. We know already that there is a new intensity to the way in which fans think about the objects of their affection. Fans of *The X-Files* are famous for writing their own story lines, second-guessing script and directorial decisions, and otherwise "participating" in the show as if it were indeed just as much theirs as Chris Carter's.

Every show in the world of entertainment wishes for this kind of interest and support. But it is not clear that the world of entertainment has glimpsed its implications. When fans take possession of *The Simpsons* and *The X-Files*, they do precisely that. In some more than metaphorical sense, the show comes to *belong* to them and their "rights" of "ownership" must be honoured. Fans must be allowed, within the limits noted above, to work and rework materials as if these materials belonged to them.

Fox can't have it both ways. They cannot profit from the support fans give *The X-Files* and *The Simpsons*, and then deny them access to the materials that sampling demands. Corporations must choose. As the culture of commotion grows more dynamic and interactive, corporations must decide whether they are, literally, in or out. Will they make themselves an island or will they enter the mix? Making themselves an island may have certain short-term financial benefits, but the long-term costs can be substantial.

Disney has made its choice. It aggressively challenges any non-Disney treatment of its properties. But there is a risk here: that the culture of commotion, if it must, will "go around" Disney, developing other resources, engaging other things. When the corporation withholds itself from the culture of commotion, it risks the possibility that their properties will diminish in value, that they will cease to be *properties*. As it is, corporations now act as if there is no cost to "copyright fright." But as the culture of commotion demands cultural events and artifacts that allow for engagement (as opposed to merely passive reception), the traditional posture is a dangerous one. Fiercely protecting intellectual property is a way of courting obscurity, of absenting the corporation from the culture of commotion, of damaging the bottom line.

What Disney does not always see is that there is a generation of film goers who have an entirely proprietary feeling about popular culture. Their passion for a film like *Snow White* leaves them with the feeling that this property in some sense *belongs to them*. The moment the corporation declares its exclusive rights of use, it punctures this proprietary feeling, alienates the film goer, and undermines the very engagement that Disney has done so much (and succeeded so well) in creating. The proprietary sense may have no foundation in legal fact, but pity the corporation that decides to ignore it.

The impatient reader will say Disney is so powerful in its ability to create appealing sound and image, and its ability to insinuate this sound and image into popular culture, that there can be no real challengers to its current position. Certainly, no group of "kids" labouring in obscurity on the Net can hobble this power and diminish its influence. But let's remember that virtually none of the important innovations to take place in the mainstream in the last few years have emerged from the Disney studios. Once the inventor of this culture, Disney now must compete with what can happen in obscure garages and "found sound" studios. It must compete with the likes of Tarantino, Linklater, and Industrial Light and Magic.

Disney has changed. The original enterprise produced Mickey Mouse, Donald Duck, Goofy, Dumbo, Grumpy, and Pluto. It may have been borrowing from folk and contemporary culture but was still the "originator" of these now precious creatures. Can the present corporation now deliver these? What it appears to be doing instead is borrowing. What are *Aladdin*, *Pocahontas*, and *Hercules* if not a raiding of pre-existing "properties" from the public domain? (Who, pray tell, owns the copyright for *Pocahontas?*) One *Toy Story* does not perpetuate the tradition. It is not clear Disney created Mickey, Donald, and Goofy with a ruthless eye for return on investment. Walt Disney, the man, took on debt. He frequently put creative results ahead of financial outcomes. The results are a "patrimony" that is the envy of the entertainment "industry."[178]

Donald Duck, Goofy, Dumbo, Grumpy, and Pluto

Three things are clear. One, the new Disney corporation may no longer evidence the creativity on which its fortunes are founded. Two, the world outside the corporation teems with creative energy and experimentation that were once Disney's special contribution to contemporary culture. Three, "consumers" of the Disney "product" are increasingly *participatory* in their expectations of the world of entertainment. They possess the creative energy and experimentation Disney must muster for itself. (It's as if the spirit of Disney has shifted from inside the corporation to outside the corporation.) Surrounding itself with the great wall of copyright in these circumstances is perhaps not the wisest thing to do. Surely, Walt Disney, the man, would have had second thoughts — and more interesting solutions.

I am *not* arguing that Disney can only find originality outside itself or that it must turn to its fans to create its "product." I am *not* arguing that Disney has no right to control the creative accomplishments of its studios or that it must hand over its inventions to all and sundry. I am arguing merely that Disney is no longer the great centre of creativity it once was and that, perhaps, no corporation can be. I am arguing merely that the world now teems with inventive powers previously undreamed of. Everyone has creative powers and technologies that were once Disney's relatively exclusive domain. In such a world, détente is a good idea and something like active interpenetration is an even better one.

shackle the dogs

The very distinction between "producer" and "consumer" in the culture of commotion is blurring. Consumers will not suffer the passivity of staring in wonder at the silver screen.[179] In the longer term, they may actually refuse entertainment they have not been allowed to help produce. That time is still a few years off, but Disney may find itself forced to choose how it will treat its fans, whether to let them in or wish them goodbye. It may be time to stop listening to the lawyers. It may be time to shackle the dogs of copyright. Fortresses must fall. Partnerships may prosper.

Plenitude's Secret Agents
(in brisk review)

PLENITUDE DOES NOT FLOURISH only for negative reasons: because the forces that once held it in check are in decline. It flourishes because it has many agents at work in the world. We may think of these as agents in both Ian Fleming's and Joseph Conrad's sense because they are sometimes altogether glamorous and sometimes altogether not.

The Reformation keeps reforming. What acted first upon the Catholic church continues to act upon the Protestant one, producing a succession of low church factions. New churches are created, old ones remake themselves. In the old world, religion was, generally speaking, a brake on innovation. In the Protestant tradition, it is sometimes one of its engines.[180]

There is also the *Golden Age* reflex, the conviction that the present day is the decayed version of a better time. But, typically, what is "recovered" is not the past, but an invention of something called the past. Thus does tradition play midwife to novelty.[181]

The Romantic revolution of the 18th century is another of the ideological engines of Western diversity. As Izenberg puts it,

> [O]ne of the most distinctive features of Romantic writing is the challenge to the idea of fixed, insurmountable limits to human nature.... In breaking the boundaries of legitimate authority, the Revolution also unraveled the traditional limits (even those of the Enlightenment) that had previously confined the self.[182]

This Romantic tradition is routinely identified as a creator of new species of social life. This is the way the hippie counterculture is almost always explained.[183] But the Romantic tradition has deeper, more seditious potential. For it warrants every individual *as an individual* to seek irreproducible novelty.

What the late eighteenth century adds is the notion of originality. It goes beyond a fixed set of callings to the notion that each human being has some original and unrepeatable "measure". We are all called to live up to our originality.[184]

In the once very influential words of D.H. Lawrence,

Each human self is single, incommutable, and unique. This is its *first* reality. Each self is unique, and therefore incomparable. It is a single well-head of creation, unquestionable: it cannot be compared with another self, another well-head, because, in its prime or creative reality, it can never be comprehended by any other self.[185]

Individuals are not merely freed of social constraints. They are obliged to pursue their absolute uniqueness, to live up to their originality.

We may take one apparently trivial example here. We take for granted that every scholar will work on a unique project. If there was a time when scholars worked together as if in an *atelier*, this has largely ceased. Every scholar must be freestanding—anything else is a declaration of professional incompetence. Shils takes the uncharitable view:

The Romantic idea of originality, which claimed that genius must go its own unique way, has been transposed into one that demands that the subject matter should be unique to the investigator. This has led to much specialized triviality in humanistic research.[186]

the Romantic mission

The Romantic idea of originality is an obvious spur to plenitude. It promised an absurd reduction in which every individual is obliged to make him or herself different from every other individual. Add to this idea the more modern desire for authenticity and plenitude is redoubled. There is now a "real real" concealed somewhere in the soul/self that must be honoured, got out, made public. Authenticity adds a special urgency to the Romantic mission.

Now the self must be rescued from falsehood and error. Uniqueness will not happen along. The individual cannot expect to have it thrust upon him/her. It is something to be divined, sought out, fought for, and otherwise taken by special effort. Now plenitude is not merely allowed, not merely enjoined, but positively glorified as a triumphant enterprise.[187]

But there is no single ideological mother lode of diversity. The prompts for plenitude are everywhere. Berlin characterizes Mill's passion for it:

> [W]hat [Mill] came to value most was neither rationality nor contentment, but diversity, versatility, fullness of life—the account of individual genius, the spontaneity and uniqueness of a man, a group, a civilization. What he hated and feared was narrowness, uniformity . . . he set himself against the worship of order or tidiness. . . .[188]

worship

The ideas that establish this new warrant for diversity are themselves multiple and diverse. Take, for instance, the notion of relativism. It has a *range* of supporters. In the disapproving words of Allan Bloom,

> Some [students] are religious, some atheists; some are to the Left, some to the Right; some intend to be scientists, some humanists or professionals or businessmen; some are poor, some rich. They are unified only in their belief in relativism. . . .[189]

The rise of relativism has served plenitude variously, with one particular advantage. It helped diminish moral disapproval. As long as the mainstream could rely on the irradiating power of disapproval, it could control and destroy innovations of every kind. But now we disapprove of disapproval. Now we wither withering. Every first-year sociology student is instructed in the cruelties of labelling, marginalizing, stigmatizing.[190] We take for granted that the hostile gaze, snort of derision, ridiculing remark, the cutting "tssszh" are beneath us. This relativism has helped plenitude enormously. Beneath this gentle trade wind, new species flourish.[191]

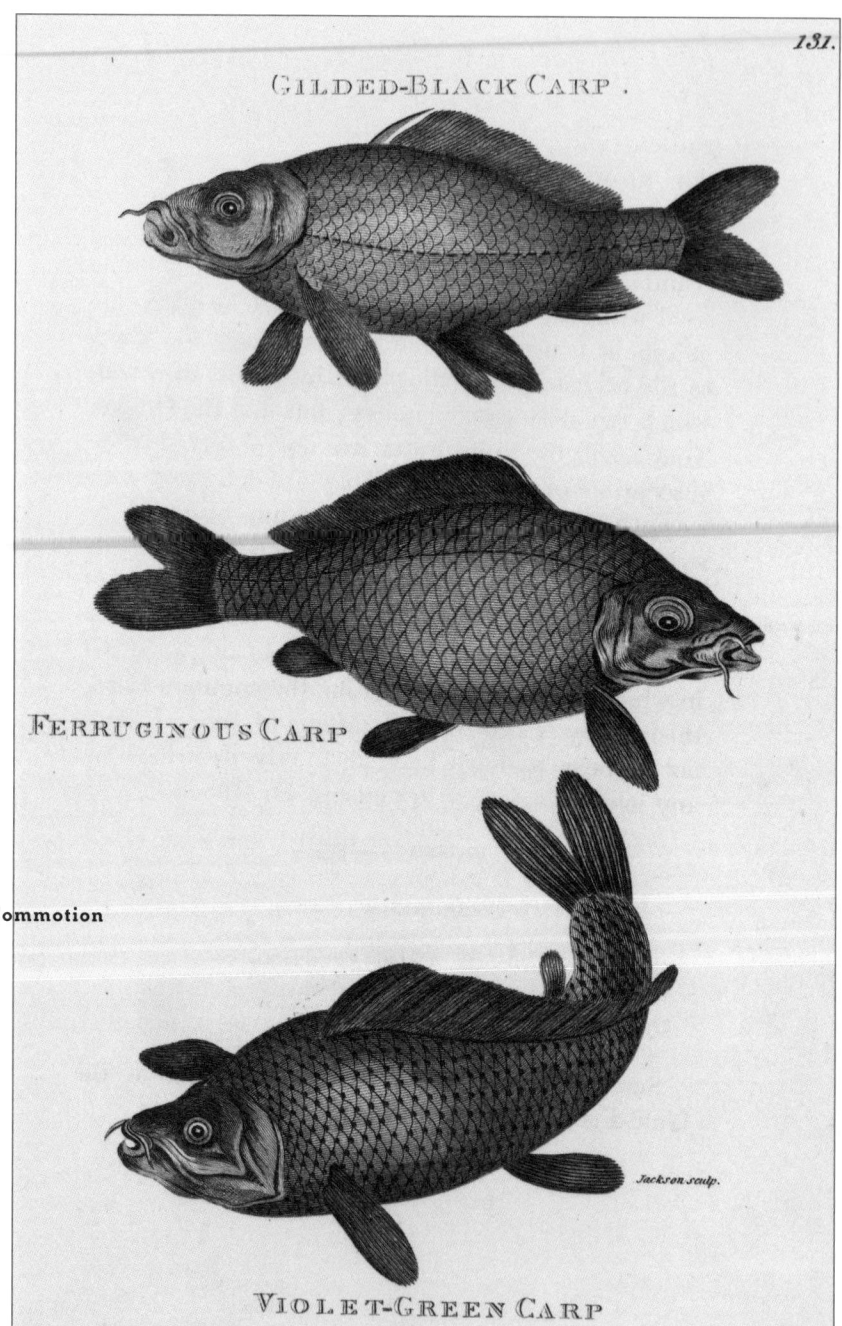

GILDED-BLACK CARP.

FERRUGINOUS CARP

VIOLET-GREEN CARP

Jackson sculp.

Plenitude's Fellow Travellers
(in brisk review)

———————

So much for the "great idea" influences. There are more modest and more practical ones, closer to home. There was a time when our culture exhibited a strong centre-periphery pattern of control.[192] There were a few great centres of cultural creativity: London, Paris, New York, for instance. So strong was the hegemony of these centres that until very recently we could *not* be a truly influential fashion designer outside of Paris.[193] We could not be an important American filmmaker outside of Los Angeles or New York. It didn't matter how good we were. Trends came from trendmakers, and trendmakers came from centres of influence.

The great centres have been displaced a little. In the last 15 years we have seen important cultural innovations emerge from Atlanta, Seattle, and Minneapolis. In a global village, even Hong Kong, Bombay, Bristol, and Lund can have an influence. This makes the system vastly more difficult to control. The gatekeepers may, for instance, control the production studios of Los Angeles but they were relatively powerless to control the garages of Seattle in the late 1980s. The great masters of *haute couture* may control the resources and prestige of Paris, but now they have no choice but to compete with the innovations of Milan and Tokyo.

The continual shift from rural to urban has been a powerful inducement to plenitude. Robert Park, the great observer of this phenomenon, remarked, " ... a smaller community sometimes tolerates eccentricity, but the city often rewards it."[194]

What cities do not reward, they may still encourage through benign neglect. As long as city dwellers satisfied certain minimum requirements of public life, they were free to do as they wanted. Furthermore, the city offered up a moving feast of inspiration. With their steady stream of reward, neglect, and inspiration, cities steadily turned some difference into more difference.

The very idea of the "gatekeeper" is at risk. There was a time when we could talk, as Lynes did, about the "taste makers," arbiters of how people lived.[195] This is now difficult. The person who can mobilize attitude and invent, in the process, a new "life-style" or "gender" or "political faction" can come from virtually anywhere. They can be film directors (Richard Linklater), radio personalities (Rush Limbaugh), journalists (Tom Wolfe), real estate salesmen (Werner Erhard), ice cream executives (Ben and Jerry), housewives (Martha Stewart), fashion designers (Vivian Westwood), film stars (Johnny Depp), Missouri preachers (Joyce Meyer), or fitness instructors (Susan Powter).[196] These decisions are no longer made on high by polite society. Less and less are they made by one of our competing elites or by experts. They are no longer made at the carefully monitored centre of our society. They can now come from "nowhere."

fitness instructors

Marketing, as we have seen in the "Withering Still" section, can be a force for conformity. But it is also an agent of diversity. It is an important agent of plenitude because it does not care about the wishes of any magic circle of experts or moral leaders. Advantage belongs to those who can "play back" new trends as accurately and quickly as possible. The innovation that begins in a small corner of California (South Central Los Angeles, say) is up and into the world very quickly. No sooner have African American kids there invented a new dance step than it finds its way into a soft-drink commercial and the affections of white middle-class kids living in the suburbs—in Chicago and Prague.[197]

What makes the intellectuals and church leaders so unhappy is that marketing does not edit or censor. It does not decide that Snoop Doggy Dog might be too violent an influence on American teenagers. It does not wonder about the effect John McEnroe might have on national standards of etiquette. It does not ask whether skateboarding is a decorous addition to city life. It grasps at them, whatever they are, and makes them legion. Into the world—into advertising—into the world.

But marketing has more creative powers as well. The jogging craze of the 60s, 70s, and 80s certainly felt like an original idea to the millions who participated in it. But it occurred largely at the prompting of a Nike founder and Oregon track coach Bill Bowerman. And with jogging came a larger, more important change: the deprofessionalization of sports activities. At Nike's bidding, a nation of couch potatoes turned to fitness. This did not have much to do with what was happening in New York City or Washington. Certainly it had nothing to do with our physical education teachers or the inspiration of 50-year-old Swedish health enthusiasts. It was largely "Just Do It" that did it.[198] The marketplace is not merely a relay station for innovation. It is sometimes its very origin.

The very idea of the *mass* market is now, as we have noted, in some question. New production technologies and management models make it possible for companies to speak to a diverse universe. Seiko makes some 3,000 styles of watch, Philips some 800 models of TV. There are more than 100 varieties of Walkman. Jelly Belly makes some 40 different flavours of jelly bean with instructions on how you may combine certain flavours to produce still more. There was a time when the consumer society forced monolithic definitions of the consumer. This is no longer necessary. And now that it is no longer necessary, the marketplace helps create still greater diversity.[199]

The transition from broadcasting to narrowcasting is germane. Three monolithic networks give way to many more smaller ones. We are now looking at television productions that have the scale of the pirate radio station — one person and a camera.[200] And if the promise of the Internet is fulfilled, things will expand exponentially. Steven Levy argues that the "media monopolists" (Disney, CBS, Westinghouse, Ted Turner, Bell Atlantic) have lost control of the 500-channel universe. In its place we can expect 500 *million* channels, a limitless universe of "propeller heads" over which the monopolists have less control.[201] This will be one of the great battles of the next decade: media concentrations on one hand, and Internet decentralization on the other. It is now too close to call.

Ted Turner

The Internet is potentially a great agent of plenitude because of its capacity to provide "critical mass" for interests that would otherwise languish in obscurity. There once was a time when a 14 year old in Tacoma, Washington, who happened to have a passion for his new skater-gothic-propeller-head fusion was a voice in the wilderness. He could count on being a short-lived minority of two (and this only if he persuaded his little brother to go along). Now the Tacoma enthusiast can find and interact with every other 14 year old who thinks the fusion holds some interest. The minority of two can critically mass at several hundred. The skater-goth-propeller-head fusion can "take."

Journalists are agents of plenitude as well. They create a hothouse that sustains even the most fragile new species. Tom Wolfe and Hunter S. Thompson helped create the 60s with strategic observations. As we have noted, Wolfe actually helped define the beginning of the 80s with *The Right Stuff* and then helped accomplish its cessation with *The Bonfire of the Vanities*. Peter York discovered the "Sloan Street Ranger." *Wired* recently declared the birth of the "Zippies" and *Paper* the "D Generation." The *Geraldo* and the *20/20* staff dream of the big find: a new social species of their very own. No 19th-century naturalist worked harder in the tall grasses of Africa or the rainforests of Brazil. *Newsweek* recently announced "an epochal moment in American sociology, the birth of a new class." (This is a particularly addled example. *Newsweek* did not discover a new class but merely the rise of a new generation to an old one.)[202]

This coverage has its own hothouse effect. Press coverage brings new members — even when the coverage is unsympathetic. According to MacKenzie, many transgenderists and cross-dressers report their first "coming out" experience was inspired by TV talk shows, however sensational and damning.[203] This may be called the *New York Times* restaurant review effect: even bad reviews are good for business.

The fashion system does not work as it once did. Once, what came into fashion was obliged to go out of fashion. The old was forced out by the new. But fads and fashions no longer seem as thoroughly discredited by their fall from grace. Even platform shoes can stay in circulation. It's as if we are surrounded by the archaeological accumulation of all the styles of life we ever cared about. They can come again, and they do.[204]

What is true of the fashion system seems also to be true of our moral system. There was a time when ideas that had been discredited went away and stayed away — or at any rate they went so far underground that they were effectively removed as credible positions in public discourse. No longer. Even the most hideous and repugnant of ideas burst into life. As we have seen, monsters roam the land.

Culture by Commotion

Skinheads with Nazi sympathies have recruited widely in Europe and North America. Of all the ideas in the postwar world, this one seemed most likely destined for extinction. But it flourishes.

Heroin was the object of a long and powerful campaign designed to discredit it. The campaign was largely successful. When the children of the middle class took to drug use in the 1960s, heroin was usually an unthinkable choice. With the exception of the Velvet Underground set in New York City, the world steered clear. But heroin use is now spreading among the middle class. Once unthinkable, it is a new drug of choice.[205]

heroin

There is something deeply discouraging and frightening about this aspect of the culture of commotion. Heroin and racism are not like smallpox, after all. It turns out they can't be eradicated. Our confidence in perfectibility is tested. Increasingly, there seem to be large parts of the world we no longer control or even understand. This is why, surely, we are sometimes drawn to medieval, noir, and other non-Enlightenment visions of the world, as represented by films like *The Fisher King*, *Reservoir Dogs,* and Baz Luhrmann's thoroughly Elizabethan *Romeo and Juliet*. These aesthetics *presuppose* a world that is, in places, out of control and beyond understanding. Some of the things that rise up and live on in plenitude's protean stew of contemporary culture are distinctly discouraging. We thought we'd made them go away. Now we know they never will.

enlightenment

Interestingly, even the radical agents of change appear to help sustain the old ideas. It is now a common practice among marginalized groups (blacks and gays, for instance) to "reappropriate" the language of their marginality. Thus do discredited terms like "nigger," "fag," "dyke," and "queer" return to usage. Madonna has made a career of reviving once discredited visions of femaleness. Her "boy toy" rehabilitation of Marilyn Monroe is the most famous case in point. It is as if nothing gets "read out" of discourse anymore — not by the cruel hand of fashion, not by radical groups, not by the force of collective disapproval. In the culture of commotion, everything lives on.

boy toy

There is also a contrariness at work in the world. This has been true for mass culture at least since the rise of the Beat subculture after World War II. People want to go where they are told they can't.

Indeed, the best way to create a new subculture is to declare something off limits. The moment someone insists that, say, "water worship" is an abomination, all the world prepares for a trip to the coast. In an *Alice in Wonderland* world, prohibition has no hope of preventing plenitude. It is now an act of provocation.

There is also a certain, and healthy, "uppityness." No one will accept anyone else's designation of who they are and where they stand in the social order of things. Certainly, no one will endure being placed at the bottom of society. This is the effect noticed in the literature on "cliques," that groups that feel themselves excluded or diminished will immediately deconstruct the values that treat them so. Add to this the "rituals of rebellion" studied by the Birmingham group and it is clear that there are sometimes compelling structural reasons for our contrariness.

Rising insecurity and unpredictable economics have also made their contribution. There was a time when middle-class people could entertain certain expectations about "getting along in the world." This encouraged a certain conservatism. No one was prepared to take irretrievable risks. No one had to. Something would come along. The trick for these privileged groups was "risk management."

This distinguished them from people from backgrounds of profound disadvantage. The kid from the slum had one chance, a career in boxing, so he invested everything there, holding nothing back, even when boxing would eliminate other possibilities. He had less to lose from what the sociologists naively call "overcommitment." Privation, insecurity, doubtful prospects made it sensible to "risk it all."[206]

But many (even members of the once safe middle class) have joined this world of instability and uncertainty. They abandon traditional strategies of "risk management." Individuals no longer seek to keep their "options open," for these options are dwindling. Sometimes, there is as much to be *lost* from moderation as gained from it. The "big risk" is no longer unthinkable. People who would never have dreamed of joining the circus are now prepared to consider even Cirque du Soleil.[207] This brings a vastly larger group of people into the fizzing demimonde. The protective bastion of middle class life is broken open.

PLENITUDE IN SUM

- *there is an increasing number of social species*
- *there is substantial depth to each new species*
- *there is substantial difference between the new species*
- *plenitude is aided by a delinkage of natural and cultural categorie*s
- *cross talk: plenitude provokes plenitude* across *categories*
- *cross talk: plenitude provokes plenitude* within *categories*
- *there can be speciation that marks the end of speciation*
- *plenitude is opening up and over-running the traditional domains of age and gender*
- *plenitude is opening up and over-running the domain of life-style*
- *the new species of plenitude are genuinely new and not derivative*
- *plenitude creates temporal cultures*
- *some kinds of plenitude appear designed to let us contend with plenitude*
- *but plenitude appears to be over-whelming even these lingua franca plenitudes*

- *plenitude is multiplying history, poetry, fashion, art, music, scholarship, and nationality*
- *there has been a withering of plenitude's institutional witherers: family, education, status*
- *there has been a withering of plenitude's ideological witherers: science, religion, government*
- *there are institutions that are withering plenitude still: work, sports, marketing, and Disney™*
- *plenitude's secret agents:*
  alternative religion
  golden age "revivals"
  romantic revolution
  relativism
- *plenitude's fellow travellers:*
  collapse of the centre
  expansion of the city
  decline of the gatekeeper
  the power of marketing
  transition from broad-
  to narrowcasting
  Internet
  journalism's hunt for new life
  the fashion system
  maintaining marginality
  risk and the middle class

89

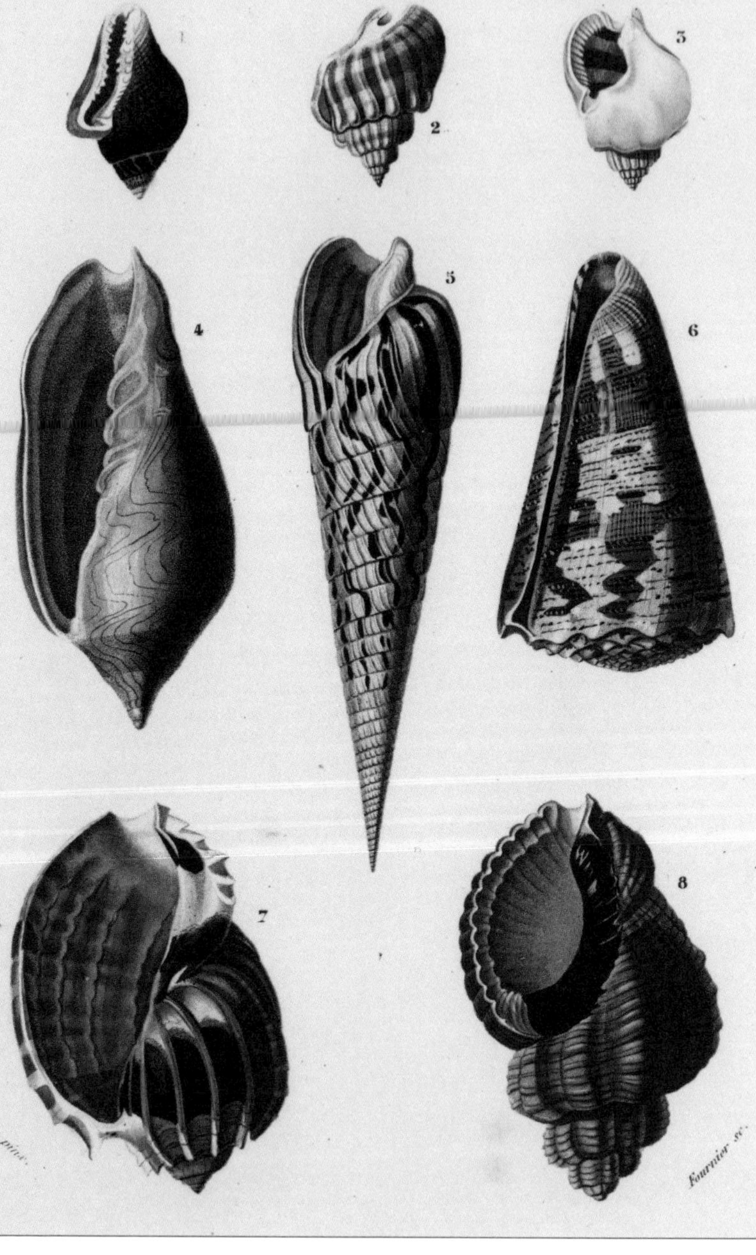
1
2
3
4
5
6
7
8
Prêtre pinx.
Fournier sc.

The Use and Abuse of Plenitude

THE INTELLECTUALS

Henry James returned to Boston looking for what he called "New England homogeneous."[208] He was greeted instead by "multiplication, multiplication of everything . . . multiplication with a vengeance." He was first horrified and then disdainful. But he was also plainly drawn to the sheer difference around him, and he claimed to detect the beginnings of a movement away from order, away from the "old presumptions and conceivabilities."[209] Few of his peers were open to such a thing. For them, the matter was clear. Difference came from the presence of an "unwashed immigrant horde" pouring into the New World. Plenitude was really just the effect of unpleasant outsiders. Hierarchy would absorb them or exclude them — making short work of plenitude one way or another.

The second generation of intellectuals managed to misplace plenitude altogether.[210] Both Whyte and Riesman warned that postwar society was exacting deference from the individual in the form of thoroughgoing conformity. Whyte showed the more delicate touch, acknowledging tensions between group and individual as well as an unexpected diversity of life in the suburbs,[211] but Riesman was simply dazzled. He found an entire and growing category of conformists, the "other-directed" character type. This group, he claimed, was so addicted to accommodating the wants of others, it could not risk departures of any kind.[212]

This notion was picked up and played back in the popular literature of the time. Here is the detective novelist, John MacDonald, a champion, one might have thought, of popular culture:

> The incomparably dull track houses, glitteringly new, were marching out across the hills, cluttered with identical station wagons,

identical children, identical barbecues, identical tastes in flowers and television. You see, Virginia, there really is a Santa Rosita, full of plastic people, in plastic houses, in areas noduled by the vast basketry of their shopping centers. But do not blame them for being so tiresome and so utterly satisfied with themselves. Because, you see, there is no one left to tell them what they are and what they really should be doing.[213]

It may well be that the 1950s *was* a time of conformity and that these scholars (and practitioners) are merely reporting the society in which they lived. (It is just as possible they had internalized one of the myths the 1950s liked to tell about itself.[214]) But the great conformist warning continued to spring from scholarly pens well after the 1950s. In the late 1960s, the redoubtable Northrop Frye was asserting: "If we look at the civilization around us, the evidence for uniformity is as obvious and oppressive as the evidence for the rapid change toward it."[215]

radar

In the early 1970s, Daniel Boorstin was proclaiming the terrible "thinning" of the American experience.[216] Deeply alarmed, intellectuals believed real plenitude (James's "multiplication of everything") could not happen. They did not see it coming, they did not think it possible. The radar screen, to use just any old cold war metaphor, was blank.

By 1978, Lasch was prepared to concede that the 1950s warnings of conformity appeared "premature."[217] The intellectuals were coming round. But the encounter was not a happy one. Like generations before them, these intellectuals treated the rise of plenitude as something that threatened order and good government, and they reacted with a kind of appalled fascination. How could this be happening? Sennett, Bell, and Lasch glimpsed the sheer power of diversity, and their thinking took an eschatological turn. They heralded what Long aptly calls a "spectre of social disintegration."[218]

Bell, the most gifted of these observers, summoned, as we have already noted, two kinds of individualism: one instrumental, the other expressive. The latter put him in possession of exactly the theory he needed to account for innovation in the social sphere. It gave him a place to begin his study of plenitude. But it was not to be. Apparently, the anxiety of the moment was more than he could stand, and Bell took refuge in the conviction that only a return to religious piety could save us from the new disorder.[219]

Lasch offered a Hobbesian account. He suggests that the American cult of competitive individualism has slid into something crueler and less rule-bound to become a "war of all against all."[220] The pursuit of happiness had also ended badly, in a narcissistic preoccupation with the self. Plenitude had created threats on every side: feminism, homosexuality, therapies of every kind, consumerism, a corrupted family, and an education system that cares nothing for history, tradition, experts, or authority. All of these, in Lasch's view, were symptoms of decline, confusion, and corruption. Plenitude was not merely inassimilable. It was a threat.

therapies

The intellectuals have reacted with shouts of alarm and indignation. They have treated plenitude as if it were an immigrant newcomer, as something crass, dangerous, reckless, and rude. This is the way high-standing groups have always stigmatized low-standing ones. It is a little shocking to see it used by those who claim, generally, to stand higher still and to be above such things as class disdain.[221]

Here is a typical rant from a badly frightened intellectual. Robert Fulford is reacting to one of the more horrifying and monstrous of the cults thrown off by plenitude, Heaven's Gate. Notice that, without a theory of plenitude, he has no way of thinking about the origin or causes of the cult. He can only resort to the notion that we have lost touch with reality, that we are the hapless victims of a delirious popular culture. This is the patrician complaint. The world is now too vulgar, too popular, too removed from the values of the intellectual, to know what it is doing. We have given ourselves over to "confusion."

a typical rant

> Whatever the cause [of the Heaven's Gate suicides], many of our fellow citizens live in a place where fantasy and reality can't be separated. They nourish themselves on a stew of undigested ideas and ill considered notions. Rock videos are the perfect emblems of this world view—bargain basement surrealism designed not to be understood by anyone, even those who produce it. Our society glories in, and profits from, confusion.[222]

Well, yes, it is all a little confusing, especially if we begin with the conviction that no one understands rock videos, not even their authors. But we know perfectly well what a rock video is. There is a substantial literature here.[223] We know the makers of rock videos are witting and sophisticated, and that they know precisely what they are doing. Fulford has apparently not heard of two particularly gifted Canadian creators of the form, Jeth Weinrich and Floria Sigismondi.[224] And we know precisely for whom rock videos are made, the cultural logic by which they are made, and, not least, how rock videos serve as cause and consequence of plenitude.

The intellectuals have cultivated the very bad habit of contradicting themselves on this topic. They insist that popular culture is a thing of no account, so driven by superficial or merely mercenary motives that it can have no real substance or significance in the world. They then insist that popular culture is the cause of one (if not all) the things that trouble us in the contemporary world. They cannot have it both ways: popular culture either means something dreadful (Heaven's Gate!) or it means nothing at all.

I include the text of an e-mail I recently sent to the Evan Solomon, editor of *Shift Magazine*. Solomon recently ran an editorial statement on the dynamism of contemporary culture that drew the following words from Fulford: "In the long history of human foolishness, has anyone ever packed more nonsense into 40 words?"

Dear Evan,

I noted Fulford's savaging of *Shift* in the pages of the *Globe and Mail* today.

Surely, seven things are clear:

1) A generation of intellectuals, academic and journalistic, routinely mock and marginalize those who would take popular culture seriously.

2) These intellectuals routinely identify popular culture as one of the causes of our present confusion. (Fulford appears to think there might be a connection between rock videos and the Heaven's Gate suicides! Time to stuff a little extra tinfoil in your hat, Robert.)

3) Naturally, there is a contradiction here. Either popular culture is too frothy and unimportant to be taken seriously, or it is a

cause of things like Heaven's Gate. The standard of debate here is so shot through with prejudice the contradiction bothers no one — least of all the well insulated Mr. Fulford.

4) These intellectuals have created an intellectual climate in which it is not acceptable to study or to specialize in popular culture. Try getting a degree in the topic in Canada — despite the fact that student demand is astronomical. Try getting a teaching position in what is the hottest area of academic publishing. (More contradiction.)

5) These intellectuals come from every point on the ideological continuum. Conrad Black and Rick Salutin ... finally something in common![225]

Conrad Black

6) Many of your readers are unemployed or underemployed precisely because this topic has been refused credibility. This reminds me a little of the generation of 19th century English university students who had difficulty finding employment because they had had the bad sense to study that new and exotic field called "biology."[226]

Conrad Black

7) There is a Canadian angle on this topic to the extent that Canadian culture was for awhile dressed up as high culture,[227] but the problem runs throughout the Western world. (Conrad Black and Hilton Kramer are, on this topic, the same man.[228])

Intellectuals and the Occupational Exile of a Generation
I believe that intellectuals and journalists have routinely mocked and marginalized popular culture (which is, for the purposes of this discussion, the stand-in for plenitude — if we dismiss the first, we conceal the second). And they have succeeded. Despite extraordinary student demand, there are very few programs devoted to its study in North America. Typically, students can only get at popular culture "the long way round," by entering programs of communications, film studies, or American studies that are only sometimes the best disciplinary context for study.

They have succeeded in a second hegemonic exercise. They have seen to it that popular culture has been refused the status of a serious professional interest. This is odd and unfortunate. To understand the history, substance, and theory of popular culture is almost a necessary condition of working effectively in the contemporary world. And yet a range of professionals are never given instruction in it. Journalists, lawyers, social workers, psychologists, psychiatrists, entertainers, marketers, administrators, filmmakers, media executives, teachers, policy analysts, and politicians depend on a mastery of the world around them. But they receive no instruction. They can find no instruction. On this question, everyone is an autodidact or a dinosaur. Worse, the generation of university graduates who have made the topic a private study suffer occupational exile. The very ones who have mastered popular culture are routinely excluded from positions that would allow them to make this knowledge available to the world.

Surely, every school of law should have an expert in popular culture. Surely, every faculty of social work, business school, medical school, and journalism school should have one, too. How can these programs presume to prepare their students without someone on staff who actually knows something about the structure, the process and the present state of popular culture? Surely every large public and private organization (i.e., every school board, board of health, department of social services, advertising agency, editorial board, and national brand) should have an expert on the topic, someone who can help the organization respond to changes as they take place. More important, these experts can give advance warning of new developments so that response is less belated and ad hoc. The *need* for experts in this field is, I think, unmistakable. The puzzle is why they are so few. The puzzle is why there are so few formal training opportunities and professional positions. This is the work of a senior generation who have scorched the ground they occupy. They don't much understand popular culture. They are making sure no one else does either.

Culture by Commotion

COMPLEXITY THEORY

Complexity theory ought to be useful here. In a now fabled gesture, the Santa Fe Institute brought together a team of physicists, biologists, and economists to address a new and vexing intellectual problem: how to take account of highly dynamic, changeable, spontaneous systems. How could you grasp systems that were in their very nature multiple, generative, unstable, and apparently unpredictable?

complexity theory

messy

It was an engagement with the counterintuitive. Pre–Santa Fe, theory despised messiness; analysis sought to "burn it off." Post–Santa Fe, intellectuals were prepared to *live* with messiness. It was an ineluctable property of the world. No amount of analysis could make it go away. It was, paradoxically, the new order of things. The question was: How could you construct a theory of messiness? How could you model systems that broke the rules of system?[229]

The Santa Fe approach is designed generally to apply to natural phenomenon: flocks of birds, computer simulations, and, at a stretch, economics. It was not designed to take account of human behaviour and communities. But it holds some hope for these purposes. Our society is "messy" in just the way the complexity theorists use this term. Our social "system" is generative, unstable, and unpredictable. We may have moved through what Santa Fe fellow Stuart Kauffman calls the "phase transition" and are therefore destined to "become supercritical and explode outward."[230]

Here is Kauffman on complexity theory in the field of evolutionary biology:

> Why all of a sudden do you get all this diversity? Maybe you had to get to a critical diversity to then explode. Maybe it's because you've gone from algal mats to something that's a little more trophic and complex, so that there's an explosion of processes acting on processes to make new processes. It's the same thing as in the economy.[231]

And the same thing in society. There is great diversity. And there is interplay as social species react to one another. It is not clear what the prime (in Santa Fe language, "autocatalytic") movers are, nor whether and how higher orders of integration can be achieved. But all the dynamism, the diversity, the interaction effects are here. (Surely, it would be very odd, in the larger scheme of things, if they were not.)

But finally, complexity theory proves not to be "emergent" after all. For our purposes, nothing comes of it. Promising first statements do not mature into a theory that can help us understand plenitude. Much of this failure occurs perhaps because scientists typically began by assuming "structure" and must now struggle to understand "event." On the social science side, the structuring power of event was never quite so counter-expectational, never quite so far from the theoretical apron of operations.[232] Here (and only here) scientific theory needs to catch up with certain commonplace verities in the social sciences.

But there is a more fundamental problem. None of this theory is designed to take account of systems in which order runs through idea before entering the world. There is, in other words, no allowance for the interpolating effects of intentions, ideologies, concepts. The Santa Fe account of system has a pre-Durkheimian, pre-Weberian character to it—it does not allow for culture. John Holland begins to approach the issue when he says, "*All* complex, adaptive systems— economies, minds, organisms—build models that allow them to anticipate the world." But finally his account of adaptive systems turns on a behaviourism from which culture is excluded.[233]

Most troubling is the Santa Fe inability to deal with *real* dynamism. The systems we will be observing can change not just their manifestation at any given moment, but the generative principles from which they spring. This "meta-metamorphic" reflex remains a perfect mystery from the Santa Fe point of view. We are left to wonder how social systems can change the rules of the game as they go, and how they survive the structural instabilities this opens up. Can this merely be emergent? Or are there, perhaps, first principles that allow first principles to be refashioned ("firster" principles, as it were)? If firster principles exist, where can they be resident? What properties must a system have to create, allow, forgive, survive this kind of operation upon itself? Are Von Neumann's self-reproduction rules enough? Shouldn't we be looking for self-transformation rules?

allow, forgive, survive

This is where the inability of complexity theory to deal with the mediating role of idea becomes especially problematical. For this, in a culture of commotion, is where firster principles must be resident.

But these complaints aside, there are tantalizing hints of illumination. Chris Langton's work in the Santa Fe tradition examines how systems hang suspended between the extremes of order and chaos:

> [R]ight in between the two extremes, [Langton] says, at a kind of abstract phase transition called "the edge of chaos," you also find *complexity*: a class of behaviors in which the components of the system never quite lock into place, yet never quite dissolve into turbulence, either. These are the systems that are both stable enough to store information, and yet evanescent enough to transmit it. These are the systems that can be organized to perform complex computations, to react to the world, to be spontaneous, adaptive, and alive.[234]

C'est nous, spontaneous, adaptive, and alive. Now for a theory that reveals how we do it. Complexity theory, it turns out, cannot help us.

SUBCULTURE THEORY

There is a small band of social scientists who study "subcultures." This concept looks promising for our purposes, but in the event it proves a frustrating exercise in self-imposed limitation. This scholarly community is interested in only certain aspects of certain subcultures. As a result, the full character of plenitude goes neglected.

Professor Brake takes the characteristic position: "Subcultures exist where there is some form of organized and recognized constellation of values, behaviour and actions which is responded to as differing from the prevailing set of norms."[235] Subcultures, these scholars tell us, develop in response to "dominant meaning systems." They are acts of resistance, protest, refusal which seek to differentiate themselves from the mainstream. Plainly some subcultures are devoted to and shaped by resistance, but to see them only in this way is a problem.[236] For the mainstream is losing its centrality. Increasingly we live in a world of coincident communities, a great swamp of possibilities. There is no *main* stream. There are many streams. The "dominant meaning systems" are coming undone. It is less and less clear what "rituals of resistance" might resist.

This is bad news for the subculture theorists. The rationale of the scholarly enterprise is disappearing. Subcultures can no longer be seen to be "pushing off" against the rest of culture. Now they can be inspired by other motives, driven by other inclinations. If the inspiration for cultural difference is no longer political opposition, what then? The "house" explanation loses its powers of illumination. The subculture theorists cannot explain line dancers, golf fanatics, bass fishermen, and other "subcultures" they have so fastidiously ignored. In the world of plenitude, it is not even clear they can explain oppositional teens.

golf

POSTMODERNIST THEORY

The postmodernists offer a way to think about plenitude. Jameson treats the topic much as Sennett, Bell, and Lasch do. He worries about the prospect of a diversity in which we find "each group coming to speak a curious private language of its own, each profession developing its private code or ideolect, and finally each individual coming to be a kind of linguistic island, separated from everyone else."[237] More recently he has expressed a very considerable irritation that the emergence of pluralism has been allowed to efface the realities of class. He is inclined to refer to the "obscene consumerist pluralisms of late capitalism" and to dismiss them as the deceptive but unremarkable residue of capitalism in its last phase.

This reproduces the flaw of some Marxist theory in the face of plenitude. Unless the groups thrown off by plenitude can be seen to reflect class realities, or unless they can be seen to be a mobilization *against* these realities, they are declared minor, mere, and/or epiphenomenal. Much of the plenitude we have examined in this book has no immediate economic basis or political significance. (It does not come from nowhere but it does not come from this.) Jameson's theory gives us grounds for two reactions to plenitude: indifference or bemusement.[238]

But it is hard to see why Jameson does not resort to his more powerful, interesting, and central argument on the insubstantiality of the contemporary world. He accepts Baudrillard's contention that ours is a "culture of the simulacrum," a place in which images relentlessly circulate, referring increasingly to themselves and becoming increasingly divorced from the validating effect of originals, authenticity, the "real," or the "true." In this culture, the structuralist "system of difference," the great grid that underwrites all meaning, comes undone and we are left living, like the schizophrenics Jameson takes to be emblematic of our age, in a "rubble of distinct and unrelated signifiers." The consumer society of late capitalism helps to intensify this ceaseless circulation of images (and their detachment from the world) through the institutions of advertising, filmmaking, and, of course, that postmodernist shrine to pastiche, Disneyland.[239]

In such a world, surely, plenitude is utterly to be expected. We should expect the categories of gender, class, age, and life-style to lift off their moorings in the postmodernist fashion and begin flashing past us in endless circulation. Why not a constant bricolage in which the fragments of the old order are endlessly assembled and reassembled in an inexorable but idle exploration of all possible permutations? And why not say that this is driven by something like the schizophrenic's anxious hope that somewhere in the endless possibilities there is one that will make enduring sense — but never, of course, the present one? What better motive for plenitude than the conviction that the present possibility must necessarily be mistaken — that one must move on? Jameson's culture of simulacrum appears purpose-built to explain the profusion of species that is the contemporary world.

The trouble is that *someone lives here*. Not without difficulty and not without confusion, but we do inhabit the worlds thrown off by plenitude. Even when we treat them as ships of brief passage or, still more merely, as navigational devices, the meanings thrown off by plenitude are engaging, sometimes even convincing ways of being. If our social species were somehow the ethnological equivalent of psy-

word salad

chiatry's "word salad," would this be possible? If our culture were truly a matter of simulacra (a world salad, as it were), our lives would make even less sense than they do. They would in fact be uninhabitable. The very complicated business of having a self, living a life, managing relationships, crafting performances and communications that others found intelligible (or at least plausible), all of this would be impossible.

These matters plainly do not trouble a Marxist professor of comparative literature. They do not intrude. But they do concern the anthropologist very much. The anthropologist is not allowed to "smuggle" in the substance of social life, nor to "give" him/herself what does not show on the surface of contemporary culture. The anthropologist is obliged not merely to observe that the bumblebee *grave problems* flies but to show *how* it does so. For the anthropologist, the postmodernist theory presents very grave problems. If the theory were true, much of social life would be impossible. Our lives would be an *lunch* exercise in constant miscommunication, misdirection, and misadven- *with a friend* ture. We would not be able to manage the relative simplicities of "lunch with a friend." We would not be able to read a "newspaper." We would not be able to construct this paragraph and we certainly could not read it. (Don't you dare.) Things are complicated, they are *not* chaotic.

There is, not to put too fine a point upon it, a certain anthropological naiveté in the postmodernist argument. Consider the dinner party in which debate might arise. Those who speak for the postmodernist side can win every point and still lose the argument — simply because the meal succeeded as a meal, simply because it did not dissolve into a food fight. Dinner (and the debate within dinner) demands shared knowledge and the execution of a large body of social rules and understandings. Consider one relatively small part: conversational "turn taking."[240] The rules of turn taking specify who may speak, for how long they may speak, how each "turn" may be requested and assumed, and how it may and must eventually then be given up. Turn taking is really a very small part of this thing called a dinner conversation, but it is nevertheless an astonishingly complicated bit of communication, the successful execution of which demands that conversation parties "process" data and judgements skilfully and on the fly. Each party to the conversation must see who wishes to speak, calculate who is entitled to speak, decide how and how forcefully to prosecute their own wish to speak, and they must make all these decisions on the basis of a streaming body of information and many rules of interpretation, the significance of which changes as the conversation does.

Grasping and executing these rules at a dinner party is not a matter of good manners; it is a *necessary condition* of communication. Without them, the meal would become competitive and then hostile. It would fail as a meal. (We would make a meal of the meal.) It would fail as a debate. If we truly lived in a world of empty signs and private languages, we would not know it: for the discourse that clarified our condition would be impossible. If we truly inhabited a "rubble of distinct and unrelated signifiers," even very simple acts of interaction would be mystifying and unsuccessful. Simple greetings would be beyond us, to say nothing of the breathtaking complexities of turn taking, to say nothing at all of the still more astonishing complexities of the simplest dinner conversation.[241]

It is easy for us to take these rules for granted. It is easy to miss their operation. But as Erving Goffman demonstrated, those who do not believe in the existence or importance of these conventions should engage in conversation with those who do not know them. In Goffman's case, this meant the tragic but instructional chaos of the "psychiatric institution." Goffman took up residence to see what became of conversation. One by one, the otherwise invisible rules of conversation came into view, as each was broken by a patient. Jameson finds illumination in the experience of the schizophrenic. Here is another opportunity for instruction.[242]

We do not experience culture as an arbitrary set of meaning-making conventions — it feels to us, most of the time, transparent to the world it constitutes for us.[243] But this does not give us licence to "see through" and so disregard the patterned quality of social life — especially at this crucial moment of analysis. Postmodernism offers several essential insights into the culture of commotion but it fails to let us account for the miracle of modern life — that even while we live in a society filling with new species of social life, we continue to function as a social world. As the Santa Fe complexity theorists would put it, we are living somewhere *between* chaos and order, *not* in the former's clutches. We need a theory that shows how the system remains a system even as systemness is challenged.[244]

This may be seen as one of the postmodernist's great theoretical insufficiencies. Messiness, or as we are calling it here, *commotion*, is as troublesome for them as it is for the modernist theories of meaning and action. The figures of speech that play such an important role in the postmodernist corpus — irony, pastiche, contradiction — allow for the *multiplicity* of meaning.[245] But they do not let us account for its emergence and continual self-transformation. The postmodernists are right to insist that we come to terms with meanings that multiply and circulate. But they do *not* let us account for how these meanings suspend themselves between order and chaos, and continue to work, more or less, as meanings. They do *not* let us account for systems that never quite lock into place but yet never quite dissolve into turbulence. They do *not* show us "firster" generative principles — indeed, they assume these away. ✳

Culture by Commotion

How Not to Think
about the Culture of Commotion

THERE ARE TWO COMMON WAYS to misunderstand the culture of commotion. One of them is to treat it as a "gusher." In this mode, the culture of commotion becomes an endlessly fecund source of novelty of which no systematic account can be given. What do Liz Phair, Bill Murray, Tricky, Ani DiFranco, and Jim Carrey have in common? We can't really say. Because we never ever try. For an anthropologist visiting from another culture, this would be the first order of business. But we are happy to see ourselves as a thing of disparate bits and pieces. We act as if each TV series, fashion designer, lunch box, beauty pageant, Christmas fad, singing sensation, and life-style experiment exists in isolation, an immaculate conception, a discrete event.

immaculate conception

We act as if popular culture were all a great heap, shot through with connections (fashion designers quoting movies quoting street kids quoting TV series quoting fashion designers), connections we love to remark upon but not to analyse. We are so enamoured of pop culture's ability to generate novelty, we simply take it for granted. We do not ask whence this generativity comes. We do not ask whether the bits and pieces might ever be pieced back together again. We've had a great fall. And that's the end of it.

On the other side, the "gill net" approach. In this mode, we seek to contain all the diversity of the culture of commotion with a single new encompassing idea. Sometimes this is a typology. Certainly they are good fun (and, sometimes, quite funny). Gail Sheehy gives us nine categories, including "Turbulent Thirties" and "Serene Sixties."[246] Michael Adams gives us 12 categories, including "Thrill Seeking Materialists" and "New Aquarians."[247] This is really too dim for words. There is too much variety for typologies to serve us, especially these. (New Aquarians! Pray, sir, what decade are you living in?) Twelve categories will not let us capture even the diversity of the world of gender, let alone the rest of the world. It does make you wonder whether these people, a journalist and a pollster, respectively, can have been paying attention. There is a certain Larry King quality to it all ("Outer space? Let's take a caller from Knoxville, Tennessee!")

But the bean counters have another strategy: the global explanation. In this case, the writer seizes on one force, one cause, one factor. This was Christopher Lasch's ill-fated inspiration when he seized upon narcissism as the explanation of the contemporary world. This is better probably that the explanation of "class" to which old-fashioned Marxists still resort. And certainly this was better than the notion of "status" in which less-gifted academics, following Veblen, used to take refuge.

But the global explanation is still a favourite intellectual pastime. Consider *Dumbing Down: Essays on the Strip-Mining of American Culture,* recently published by Norton. This collection of essays turns on two assumptions: (1) that contemporary culture is going to hell in a handbasket, and (2) that most of this can be put down to a systematic "dumbing down" process now at work in America.[248]

There is really nothing intellectuals like to do more than wring their hands and talk about the decline of national standards. It makes them feel so neglected — and important. But for them, the final collapse of civilization. But for them, the deluge. Plainly, in our moment of need, just moments before we slip beneath the flotsam and jetsam-strewn waters of contemporary culture, we will reach out for...the saving, forgiving grasp of the philosopher king. We will ask the intellectual to put things right — to save us from ourselves, to help us come to our senses and see that, really, we do need them.

getting better But *Dumbing Down* is an act of dumbing down. There is good evidence that parts of the contemporary world are getting better, not worse. Some television has improved steadily from its early "wasteland" days. The standards of production, writing, acting, and directing are now, in places, quite high; see the likes of *NYPD Blue, ER, Homicide, Frasier,* and one or two others.[249] Indeed, we have seen a certain (forgive me) "smartening up" in contemporary culture. This runs against all predictions, especially those from the hysterical Dwight Macdonald and other middleweights who built reputations by claiming prescience they did not have.[250] And it puts paid to the self-righteous condemnations of *Dumbing Down* as a global explanation.

Dumbing Down is not wrong; it is merely partial—as every global explanation of the culture of commotion must now be. In the culture of commotion, there can be no single explanation of anything. Yes, there is dumbing down. American television is, in places, getting steadily worse. No one quite believed that there was much room to fall from *The Dukes of Hazzard*, but they were wrong.[251] But just as surely, we have seen a "smartening up" unanticipated by the intellectuals. In between, there are qualities and kinds of every quality and kind. Intellectuals like the sweeping explanatory vista, but this is no longer possible in the culture of commotion. That they continue to search for it says how little they grasp the implications of plenitude. ✺

*Dukes
of Hazzard*

Culture by Commotion

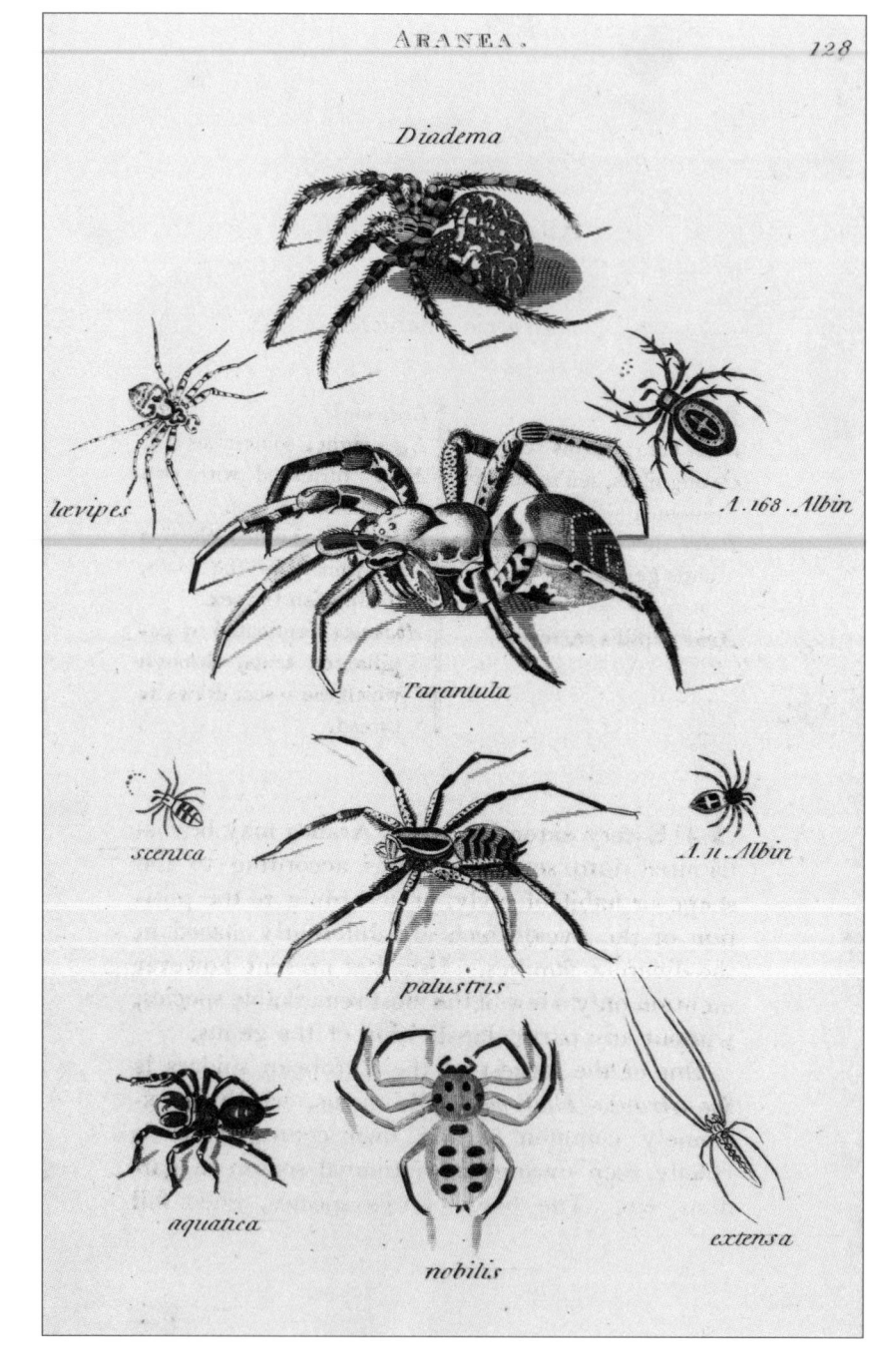

Diadema

lævipes

A.168.Albin

Tarantula

scenica

A.11.Albin

palustris

aquatica

nobilis

extensa

Politicizing Plenitude

In this section, I will show how plenitude has been taken hostage by political interests. As plenitude takes on a "hyper" quality, politicization becomes more costly. It is, I believe, time to let the hostage go.[252]

THE RIGHT AND "THINGS INDIFFERENT"

It is not hard to render an anthropological account of where the Right stands and why it stands there. There is a powerful sense that the world is going to hell in a handbasket. There is anarchic, wilful, recklessly individualistic behaviour everywhere. There is evidence that we are losing touch with our most grounding and stabilizing traditions, that any kind of kook can give us advice on private and public life.[253] The world feels tippy, puzzling, dangerous, and odd. We have lives to create, children to raise, communities to build, futures to secure. How are we to do this in a land of drive-by shootings, drugs in the playground, guns in the high school, lawlessness, godlessness, and an abiding sense that private and public security can no longer be guaranteed? How are we to do it in a land of rock videos, Madonna concerts, Mapplethorpe exhibitions, gay pride parades, and a persistent sense that the rules of gender, decorum, and politesse have fled the land? To make matters worse, efforts to deal with such a world are routinely mocked and ridiculed by mainstream press.[254]

hell
in a handbasket

Plenitude is an unsettling prospect, I think, for everyone. But for the Right it is compelling evidence that things have gone terribly wrong. A well society is a stable society: composed, self-possessed, in control of itself. By this reckoning, the constant speciation of social life is evidence of a deeper malaise. Healthy societies do not throw off a constant succession of new groups. They do not engage in constant reinvention. Plenitude, says the Right, is a sign we have lost touch with our founding traditions.

The Right has targeted plentitude as the enemy. Reverend Pat Robertson suggested that feminism "encourages women to leave their husbands, kill their children, practice witchcraft, destroy capitalism and become lesbians."[255] He declared the gay community a "pathology" and a "sickness." The Reverend Jerry Falwell somehow determined "God hates homosexuality."[256]

destroy capitalism and become lesbians

The Right is not always so unsophisticated, but it has been inclined to harbour misgivings about "outsiders." In his run for the Republican presidential nomination, Pat Buchanan called Mexicans "Jose" and emphasized each syllable of Ruth Bader Goldberg's name.[257] Teenagers are asked to forgo the typical adventures of adolescence. In the mythic vision of the Right, people live in a heterosexual, two-parent, one-marriage family, preferably in a freestanding house with a white picket fence. (These houses are freestanding, perhaps, to show the family's respect for property, individuation, and *amour propre*. The fences signify, surely, the family's intention to prevent the entry [or the exit] of James's "multiplication of everything.")

There is nervousness here—and a brute and thoroughgoing discomfort with difference.

It is as if the Right can't discriminate between difference that matters and difference that doesn't. Teen fashions, rock lyrics, and certain prime-time TV shows are not differences that matter. But with no operative theory of plenitude, the Right must dispute *every* departure from convention. Worse, it must incline to moral panic.[258] Surely some differences are, in the apposite language of the Protestant Revolution, a "thing indifferent"—in the larger scheme they do not matter. A thing indifferent makes no difference; it may be allowed to stand.

Again and again, the Right prohibits in a wide swath, where something more discriminating would do. The effect is to make the community smaller and more brittle than it needs to be, and to make the Right an enemy (real or apparent) of the expressive, creative, sensual, and open-minded. (This was the political advantage of a figure like Lee Atwater. He was "proof" that Republicans were not repressed and life-denying. P.J. O'Rourke has made a somewhat wittier contribution. Whether the "party hearty" persona is properly read in this manner is another question.) The ideological costs of error on this count are great. It gives comfort and place to those who are narrow, provincial, small-minded, and nervous — and antagonizes the rest.

Effectively the Right is arguing what it has always argued — suffer *this* and the world will come undone. "This" has been the vote for women, access to high culture for those without educations, admission to law schools and medical schools for "outsiders." "This" was always made to seem the last defence of civilization, the innovation that would send the world into a downward spiral from which recovery was impossible.

And...nothing happened. In point of fact, the threatening outsider rarely proves an agent of chaos or the beginning of the end. We have brought virtually all these differences on board, and nothing changed. Civilization did not cease. We will invent many more differences and these will prove absorbable too. The world of plenitude is as accommodating as it is generative. And the voice of grave and magisterial caution is almost always wrong. Admitting the "wrong" type of people never makes the world come undone.[259]

The Right deals with messiness and commotion badly. It lives in fear of it. It suffers the debilitating illusion that small-town moralities are the way to contend with the challenges of the contemporary world. Because it cannot grasp how much of plenitude is "a thing indifferent," the Right allows itself to be taken hostage by the small-minded and the life-denying — radical Christians and young fogies both.

One does not need to be a political strategist of any great cunning to see that this bodes ill. As the world becomes more various, not just on the margin but at the centre, the party that turns its back on difference asks for trouble. And the world *is* becoming more various. And it does so in the very dens, bedrooms, and basements of the most middle-class homes in the most Republican suburbs. The Right has relied on the press of the market, the rigours of instrumental individualism, to force a certain conformity of outlook and self-expression. But, as we have noted above, even this domain is slowly opening up and cannot be relied upon to level differences forever. The last great cause for conformity is giving way. The Right will shortly lose the last factor that allows it to escape the consequences of its naiveté.

Naturally, the Right has its *own* account of plenitude. Here is William Bennett on his Washington stay as secretary of education:

> My wife Elayne and I...enjoyed wonderful evenings at the John F. Kennedy Center for the Performing Arts...but we were also on more than one occasion dismayed by some of what we saw at this revered center of Washington cultural life.[260]

good art, good music and good books

Here, and where he talks about "good art, good music and good books" that will "elevate taste and improve the sensibilities of the young," Bennett betrays a wish to see the world as exemplary. And he betrays a nervousness that the stage might be used for art that is at odds with higher values. In this world, there is a single set of things to revere and the purpose of art is to encourage us in this reverence. Art that departs from lifting hearts and minds, the gaze, to higher, nobler goals is "dismaying."

In this world, the art of Robert Mapplethorpe, for instance, is an outrage. But Bennett's difficulty is self-made. It is *only* when art is supposed to have an elevating moral purpose that Mapplethorpe's work is scandalous. Bennett is right, I think, on many points and especially when he insists that we are a culture, a civilization, with its own traditions and standards. He is right to insist that we preserve these traditions. He is right to say we mustn't make ourselves so accommodating of the values of others that we are unable to honour and realize our own. The trick is to see that plenitude is our tradition. It is one of the traditions of which we have the right to be most proud—not just the ability to endure differences, but the ability to make them. The continual creation of difference, variety, and novelty may be a signature gesture of our culture. It is most certainly a defining characteristic as we enter the next century. This is the tradition that we must honour.

No return to classical simplicities will make plenitude go away. No purifying moral purpose will make art more fit for Washington cultural life. Art is already quite slow and confused enough in its response to the varieties of contemporary life. To devote it to the celebration of an exemplary would simply remove it from usefulness altogether. More important, to devote any political capital to the task of criticizing Mapplethorpe or controlling the public venues in which his work might be seen is ludicrously mistaken. This art is a thing indifferent.

Mapplethorpe

Pity the Right such a world. For this is the wrong landscape from which to take one's lessons, the wrong one on which to stake one's ground. It is better, wiser to look to the great tutor of plenitude, city life. Cities tell us that plenitude is inevitable and that it is, within certain limits, benign. While the rural communities sought singleness, the city has always, blithely, thrown off difference and variety. The lesson of this great experiment is clear: the cultivation of sameness is not needed to secure compliance to a larger set of values. Cities work in spite of plenitude. They work because of plenitude. This is the symbolic landscape in which the real ideological lessons of the 21st century are to be found.

At the core of the Right's difficulty with plenitude is the quiet conviction that anyone who departs from convention becomes dangerous and uncontrolled. Interestingly, there is sound anthropology at work here. The second stage of van Gennep's three stages of ritual transition is the liminal one in which the individual is often seen to be a danger to him/herself and everyone around him/her.[261] But this is just the second stage of the ritual. There is a third stage, that of incorporation, in which the individual returns to the world to embrace its conventions. The Right acts as if the many groups thrown off by plenitude harbour an anarchic tendency, that people have become gays, feminists, line dancers, or Deadheads in order to escape morality. This is not the logic of plenitude. These people have reinvented themselves merely to escape *a* morality, not all morality. New

dangerous

communities set to work immediately in the creation of new moralities. Chaos does not ensue; convention, even orthodoxy, returns. Liminality is the slingshot that allows new groups to free themselves from the gravitational field of the old moralities they must escape. But liminality is almost never the condition that prevails once this liberation has been accomplished.[262]

The Right is inclined these days to declare themselves the true friends of tradition and tradition the path to civic virtue and public morality. They present themselves as champion of practices and values tested by time. But the truth of the matter is that plenitude is a Western value and indeed the very author of many of the traditions now being claimed by the Right. The Protestant traditions the Right holds so dear come out of the spirit of plenitude that created first a Church distinct from Rome and then successive, ever more radical versions of Protestantism. Plenitude was there in the beginning. A return to tradition will not make it go away. It is tradition.

Furthermore, there is nothing in plenitude in and of itself that forces a retreat from the clarity of value and morality the Right holds so dear. As Calinescu observes, drawing on Wayne Booth,

> In the monist's implicit scale of values, unity, totality, simplicity, and universality obviously rank higher than multiplicity, fragmentation, intricacy, or diversity. The scale of values of the pluralist will be tipped naturally in the opposite direction. But not necessarily so. As suggested by Booth in *Critical Understanding,* the mere assertion of plurality does not preclude the possibility of introducing some kind of hierarchy among the many interpretations (or worlds) whose irreducible existence is recognized.[263]

But there is perhaps a more pressing and personal reason for the Right to rethink their attitude towards plenitude. It is that every member of the Right must live in the world that plenitude has created for them. They must endure families that change shape and form. They must endure a workplace that is constantly reinventing itself. They must somehow manage their own lives as notions of gender change continually, as notions of the self come and go. The inhabitants of the Right must live in the world that plenitude has wrought.

They must make their peace with it. Walling themselves in a perfect little house in a charming little town will not do. This world is a fiction. It has never existed. It can never be made to exist. The wolf of plenitude has huffed and puffed and blown it all down.

What the Right needs is what we all need — the ability to shift perspectives, honour differences, embrace the generative powers of plenitude. For these generative powers cannot be diminished. They will continue to fill up the world, to work and rework the body politic so that it becomes a web of endless possibilities. New groups, entertaining new assumptions, creating new values, refusing all exclusions — these are inevitable. We need the intellectual and moral flexibility to live in such a world. There is no retreat to a single point of view. There is only movement forward into a world with many points of view.

THE LEFT AND THE PROBLEMS OF "DIVERSITY" AND "MULTICULTURALISM"

The Left has made a great deal of its sensitivity on issues of gender, race, ethnicity, diversity, and multiculturalism — a sensitivity, it typically claims, the Right cannot imagine. In fact, the Left has misapprehended and mismanaged these issues almost as consistently as the Right — with consequences every bit as grave.

The Left has not always claimed a sensitivity on this score. Plenitude was regarded by some as a barrier the revolution would have to sweep away. In the words of Gellner,

> [T]he Marxists ... thought universal and liberated man would emerge in the more tragic melting-pot of an impoverished proletariat, stripped by alienation of all specific attributes, and discovering, and implementing, true humanity through this historically imposed social nakedness.[264]

And this is how socialist regimes were often judged. They were seen to be so suppressive of difference that life was rendered, in the favourite and damning adjective, "grey." More than the common ownership, a command economy, or state culture, this was the telling detail of the socialist regimes of the 20th century, the one that condemned them most in the eyes of a not always unsympathetic West. This may not have been the most sophisticated grounds for political judgement, but for our culture, then and now, it was the most compelling. Fairly or not, we damned these regimes as insufficiently various, as enemies of plenitude.

It is only relatively recently that the Left has awakened to the possibilities of diversity. Cynical observers have said it awakened to these possibilities precisely because they were so possible. Class had proven intransigent as an opportunity to mobilize dissent outside the system or leverage power within it. Gender, ethnicity, and race looked more promising. At this moment of first curiosity, the argument goes, the Left sometimes took up the cause of diversity more for pragmatic reasons than intellectual ones.

A NARROWNESS OF DEFINITION

The first symptom of difficulty is the narrowness with which diversity is defined. The only real plenitude that counts in this scheme is that which has an explicitly oppositional quality. Thus, women's groups are "diversity," country and western line dancing groups are not. Both of these groups may equally engage the individuals within them, both may represent a very substantial shift in cultural categories and social rules, both may mark differences that will continually breed differences, but it is only when the group is explicitly at odds with the mainstream that it qualifies as interesting.

This makes for every kind of intellectual difficulty. It means that no sooner has the Left embraced plenitude as something to be taken seriously than it forswears the better part of the phenomenon. Intellectual difficulty begets political difficulty almost straight away. Earnest and pragmatic, the Left is almost always the last to know. Innovations arise, blossom, put their stamp upon the world, but it is years before the Left takes notice. Restricted to political categories, wedded to fixity, it cannot glimpse the implications of plenitude's cultural developments. This is true even of those who descend from the Frankfurt school and claim to care about contemporary culture. I expect there is no one on the Left capable of giving a good account of line dancing, this despite the fact that this world is an interesting and dynamic site for the transformation of gender, class, outlook, and, yes, politics. We may someday get such a study. But there is a good chance it will demonstrate line dancing is *really* an expression of resistance or a well-constructed instance of false consciousness. What we will *not* get is a study that begins with a simple respect for the great innovations of plenitude, something to prepare the ground before the political spade is driven in.[265]

There is a deliberate narrowness to this definition of plenitude. It is interesting to observe, for example, that the "Diversity Librarian" at the University of Michigan is responsible for collecting in the following areas: minority studies, sexual orientation studies, and multicultural studies only.[266] This so diminishes the scope of the problem as to invite astonishment. Diversity, as we have seen, overflows these categories. Real diversity happens everywhere — outside the designated political categories of the Left and its intellectual categories as well. Fully to take account of this phenomenon opens theoretical challenges and political opportunities.

But there is a more chilling aspect to the Left's notion of diversity. Too frequently, it isn't very diverse. No sooner has a gender, racial, or ethnic group been identified than it begins to get hedged in by orthodoxies and High Church rigidities. George Wolfe is writer and director of *Jelly's Last Jam*, the director of *Angels in America*, and producer of the New York Shakespeare Festival. He is both black and gay. In some communities, this definitional versatility is held against him.

Angels in America

The American thought process about pop culture is so compartmentalized that the initial impulse is to be suspicious when the scene changes. If I'm including something new, if there's a play that has a gay theme, the response is, "He not black anymore, he's doing that homosexual thing." ... I heard that there were a bunch of black people going around saying, "Oh, he's only doing that artsy, black intellectual stuff. He's not doing that *real black stuff.*" Please. So last year there were all these suspicions ... because it was mixing and matching and putting it all in one room.[267]

The same problem emerged on another score. Kristal Brent Zook has complained that the black community is also sometimes unprepared to acknowledge the feminist self. "Many in my generation intuitively understand that black women don't always think or feel or even look black in the 'authentic,' stereotypical sense of the word."[268] I do not mean to single out the African American community. In a famous article on identity politics, Todd Gitlin takes issue with "silencing" practiced by a range of groups.[269]

sight-seers There are genuine issues here that I do not want to obscure or underestimate. The task of creating a new cultural category, even in a culture devoted to plenitude, is a daunting task. New groups must labour to find a voice, a style, a concept that captures and begins then to construct a place in the world. And they must do so in the face of hostility. They must contend with the fact that existing categories are often designed to exclude from possibility (and even from the imagination) the innovation they wish to create. In the face of these challenges, the new group will be inclined, in some cases obliged, to insist on separation. It will have grounds to resent those who wander in to "take a look" — who come as sight-seers rather than the truly committed. It will have grounds to resent those who presume to steal its voice, trade in stereotypes, or otherwise misrepresent it in the general culture. There will be good grounds for vigilance and ample cause for hostility.

But plenitude is a restless creature. It will not forgive fixity. It will not endure stasis. It will not allow identity politics (or identity *scholarship*) to insist on certain orthodoxies because these are "good to think" and variously clarifying of what the emergent group might become. Plenitude resists conformity, orthodoxy, conventions, and rules. The transgressive energies out of which new groups come will continue to course through them even after the moment of creation. We cannot close Pandora's box behind us. And this is the last thing we would want to do. Plenitude is breaking through the orthodoxy imposed by a middle-class, centrist, bourgeois society, and with this change come opportunities of liberation of every kind. To resist this force is not just pointless. It is wrong.

Plenitude is a force for the infinitely divisible. It will use groups as its vehicle as long as this is possible, but it will make individuals the unit of agency the moment it is impossible. Plenitude has found a friend in individualism, and there is good evidence that it will be a lasting affair. When the Left insists on the primacy of the group over the individual, it commits an error from which there is no recovery.[270] Plenitude makes the individual the locus and an engine of much of its innovative activity. It will happily create a world that is an addition of individuals. Groups will cease to matter. Pity the ideological operation that has put groups, and especially particular groups, at the centre of the exercise.

More problematically, everyone must necessarily belong to many groups. We may be gay, but we must also be many other things. Necessarily we are only one kind of gay among many, and almost certainly we will not be that kind of gay for very long. The Left presupposes a world in which certain definitions of the individual are privileged and frozen into place. The irony is that the Left has used the idea of diversity to attack the idea of difference. This leaves it hopelessly at odds with the world plenitude has wrought.

In sum, Right and Left have not distinguished themselves on the issue of plenitude. Both of them can claim certain victories in this decade. But neither party has got this issue right. Never mind. Plenitude will have its way with them as well. ✺

Culture by Commotion

PLATE 6.

How Frightened Should We Be?

OUR WORLD IS FILLING UP with differences. And this is a good thing, for some of these differences advance the cause of human dignity. Plenitude embraces those who would otherwise be persecuted for their difference. Better, plenitude dispenses with "permission." No one needs the liberal generosity of the mainstream to exist. It is enough merely to stake out a social space and to occupy it. Plainly, this is to the good.

But plenitude should also give us pause. It has a darker side, as we have seen. It is capable of creating horrifying aberrations. Plenitude allows (encourages?) the "mustering" of paramilitary groups who cultivate their own deeply skewed notion of the world. It forgives (encourages?) a world so decentred, so without powers of withering, that even the bombing of federal office buildings in Oklahoma City can seem plausible. Plenitude permits (encourages?) the monstrous.

Oklahoma City

We have a choice. Plenitude can create the glorious or the monstrous. It depends on what we *do* with difference. It depends on what difference *becomes* for us.

Traditionally, difference has been a path to identity paved with hostility and antagonism. It has given us a "sharpener" of identity and a recipe for action: find the odd man, the odd group, the odd nation, the odd culture, and then: mock, repudiate, assault, and, too often, exterminate. (Stalin, Mao, Hitler, Amin, Pol Pot eliminated difference by eliminating people, tens of millions of them. They made our century a slaughterhouse.) *This* approach to difference has used it to sharpen identity through contradistinction. We are what the other is not. Worse, our path to definition may be found through acts of differentiation, antagonism, and hostility against the other.

Pol Pot

By this reckoning, things look rather grim. More difference can only mean more antagonism. If we are filling up with differences, we will find ourselves surrounded by *otherness* and increasingly called upon to challenge it. New and emerging identities will put our own in question. *Our* identity will depend upon the defacement of *their* identity. Plenitude's world has the potential to make us smaller, meaner, more loathing, and more loathsome. And *we* are the God-fearing folk. It will be *worse* for others, the bigots and the hatemongers. These people will find themselves so provoked by the rising tide of plenitude that any act of opposition will seem tolerable (and psychologically necessary). In the small scale, they will persevere in "fag bashing." On the large, they will target still more federal buildings.

But there is another use for difference. In this case, we use difference as a definitional opportunity. We say of otherness, "Wonder what that's like?" We venture out and try otherness on. This has always been the spirit of Mardi Gras and other liminal moments. But I think there is good evidence that our entire culture is shifting in a transformational direction. More and more, we are prepared to try on difference, to test it out.

Dennis Rodman

This is a radically new approach to difference, one that completely shifts the field of assumptions. In the old *sharpening* model, we use difference to push off against. We are not what the other is. In this new transformational model, we use difference as a definitional opportunity. We use it as a shape to try on and act out. Our most fundamental reflexes are rewired. When we see a new species of social life (Dennis Rodman, say) we no longer say, "Weirdo! Get 'em!" We say, "Um, that's pretty strange. What's it like to be like that?" We move from difference as contradistinction to difference as definition. We move from difference as sharpening to difference as shaping. Difference is less and less for "pushing off," and more and more for "trying on."

This "tilt towards transformation" is the topic of book 2 in the series. I will develop it in detail there. Here I want merely to note a double possibility. As plenitude takes hold of us, we can move in two quite different directions. We can pursue the old course, the one that uses difference as cause for alarm, hostility, and contest. We can pursue the new course, the one that uses differences as cause for transformational opportunity. Almost certainly, we will pursue both. And this too will prove, as everything seems to, yet another engine for our plenitude.

There is a second reason to be frightened. Plenitude challenges our most fundamental ideas of social and political association. What becomes of the "common good" in a body politic that has precious little in common? What happens to the "community" when it fills up with differences? How can we hope to act in concert when we are speciating so intensively and so extensively?

I wish I had a clever answer. I have what is merely a sneaking suspicion. There *is* a common culture that unites the world of plenitude. It is, I think, and this will please no one, the marketplace. This is the great lingua franca of the contemporary world. As long as we can meet somewhere in the exchange of something for the benefit of someone, we have a foundation that can sustain plenitude.[271]

I understand that this is a provocative position, and, for some, a lunatic one. There are those who say the marketplace is the enemy of plenitude and of the realization of human potential. Those who *can* endure the marketplace insist that capitalism is the problem. And those who will endure capitalism say that it is the consumer culture that is at fault. This last culprit is said to narrow choice, falsify needs, poison consciousness, blunt creativity, and block the real exploration of humanness that plenitude might otherwise make possible.

I acknowledge this argument with reservations. After all, say what you will about the marketplace, capitalism, and the consumer culture, they *have* got us this far. They have allowed for the great Cambrian explosion we see around us. Some will say that some plenitude has happened in spite of, in the very teeth of, capitalism and consumerism. Others will argue that there may be a place where the consumer culture "runs out" and that the next stage of plenitude demands its collapse. (We might argue that the "alternative movement" in contemporary music and art is best read just this way.)

But the striking thing from an anthropological point of view is that capitalism is a little like plenitude. For a great many purposes, it doesn't care (or specify) what must happen, just that something does. There was a time in the history of computers when we talked about how small was the "kernel" that a program demanded. We wanted something small and generative that could manage with as little memory as possible. In a sense, capitalism is like this. It demands relatively little space. From relatively few assumptions any number of outcomes prove possible. It is, forgive the pun, so "economical."

rules

There was a period of confusion in the history of capitalism when this was not clear. In the 1950s in particular it appeared that the marketplace could *only* work if producers and consumers participated in monstrous acts of conformity and containment. But the 1960s demonstrated the falsity of this assumption. Capitalism doesn't appear to need certain kinds of conformity. Indeed, as we enter the 1990s, capitalism appears happiest and most productive when certain conformity rules do not apply. Things that seemed essential in 1955 (e.g., what the neighbours thought) turn out to be "things indifferent."

From another point of view, one that I do not wish to obscure, this is all perfect nonsense. The economistic mentality contains a toxin that puts plenitude at risk. As long as the entire enterprise depends on a "means-end" rationality and an instrumental logic, there are

Madison Avenue

certain acts of imagination and invention that may not be allowed to happen. Just as clearly, the true creative powers of the species are held in check. The expressive potentials and the instrumental imperatives of capitalism are daily at odds with one another. They collide every time creative teams in Hollywood, Madison Avenue, Broadway, or Burbank sit down with "suits" who demand deference to the monarch ROI (as "return on investment" is called—usually without a trace of irony). To this extent, the marketplace is the enemy of plenitude. It is reductive, diminishing, and antiplenitudinous. As the phrase has it, it all comes down to money.

I accept this but I cannot ignore the fecundity I see around me. Capitalism has endured, enabled, perhaps provoked the speciation we see around us. It is, as we have noted, particularly unparticular. It doesn't care what it does. It doesn't care what we do. The strangleholds of hierarchies and elites count for less and less. And capitalism is nothing if not transformational. It is capable of astonishing cultural transformations, including, for instance, turning labour into soap, soap into solicitude, solicitude into gender, gender into society, and society back into soap.[272] And it is restless, inventive, and novelty seeking. (Or is this just the modernism within? More on this in book 3.) It throws off innovations ceaselessly. The consumer culture is a cause and a consequence of plenitude. Certainly, there are some cultural and social arrangements it will not allow. Just as certainly, there is a truly breathtaking array it will. As the phrase *might* have had it: it all comes up from money.

I do not solve this issue. But I do wish to show, in a way that social scientists (even under the influence of Simmel and Polanyi) normally do not, that capitalism is not always the villain of the piece. I wish to show that it is as often as much the agent of plenitude as its enemy. *warts* This is especially important to grasp when we are wrestling with our options in a society fully captivated by plenitude. For it is clear that as our speciation goes forward we are going to need *something*— imperfections, warts and all. Capitalism may not be a baby we can afford to lose with the bathwater.

We see already that capitalism reaches across cultures quite successfully. I do not want to ignore the horror of colonialism—only to observe that Japanese and American businessmen now routinely conduct mutually satisfactory business deals without necessarily undoing the cultural differences that exist between them. Once more, capitalism does not *care* about these differences—they are truly "things indifferent." What works across the cultures appears to be working *within* cultures—at least within the culture of commotion. As our own species multiply, we continue to have something in common. Capitalism provides the few and unspecific instructions that allow discourse to happen without specifying, within certain limits, what must transpire there.

We have reason to be frightened of the world that plenitude is constructing for us. But it is also true that there may be a net to catch us when we fall. Plenitude will continue to spin off more, and more different, species of social life, but that does not mean that we are headed to Lasch's Hobbesian war of all against all. It doesn't mean that we are headed towards a postmodernist world in which meanings collapse, evaporate, or collide. It doesn't mean that commonality cannot be fashioned. It doesn't mean that these very different species cannot work out some system of mutual recognition that leaves their differences uncompromised. The marketplace is not a perfect solution. It is never a pretty solution. It is rarely a *just* solution. But it is rather better than the alternative—a tyranny or tower of babel we can none of us survive.[273]

Finally, I think the thing we most have to fear is amnesia — our well-practised ability to forget what we know about ourselves. We come to terms with one part of the culture of commotion (what is happening to gender, say), but we forget this when we take up another part (what is happening to spiritual belief). And we forget both of these when we sit down to contemplate the tremendous innovations taking place in the worlds of scholarship, business, or art. By systematically forgetting what we know about the disparate pieces of our society, we never have to come to terms with the revolution that is taking place throughout it. Huyssen has called us a "culture of amnesia," and we are especially that when it comes to reckoning with the plenitude in our midst.[274]

The real danger is that by insisting on the partial view, by selectively forgetting what we know, we need never come fully to grips with the new realities of our world. And it is this amnesia that frightens me most. Plenitude is upon us. It will not go away. It will continue to transform everything about us. It is time to see it whole.

Culture by Commotion

Plenitude as Profession

WE CAN IMAGINE PLATO on a summer night's stroll in Athens, the air around him alive with an endless variety of winged creatures. These creatures don't always capture *our* attention (and perhaps this is because we come from a culture that is eliminating species at the rate of 25 a day). But they captured his. The sheer profusion of life. It demanded explanation and he obliged us: plenitude. A force of nature for the creation of nature.

A summer night's stroll in 1851 in England must have had something of the same effect. The English had by this time harvested certain flora and fauna into extinction, but there were still creatures aplenty. And now that Linnaeus had made it possible, the English set to discovering, naming, and classifying them with a passion.[275] Field and desk experts worked in close collaboration, the former seeking out examples, the latter finding a place for them in the great Linnaean scheme. As a shoemaker working impossibly long hours, Thomas Edward could only collect his specimens at night. He would work until dark, sleep on the spot, and collect more at dawn. Gilbert White, working without colleagues, publications, or training, made himself an exquisitely careful and accomplished observer of the natural world around him. The new field of natural history brought forward remarkable acts of self-sacrifice and scholarship.[276]

But this was not a passion for experts only. An entire nation took to the topic. Ordinary publications on the species of field, stream, and coastline were selling at the rate of 100,000 copies a week. The English so loved specimens from the seashore, they stripped parts of it clean. In the 19th century, England was very nearly a *nation* of naturalists. Almost everyone was taking part. "Every Victorian young lady, it seemed, could reel off the names of twenty different kinds of fern or fungus, and every Victorian clergyman nurtured a secret ambition to publish a natural history of his parish...."[277]

It's not as if the study of 20th-century plenitude has no precedent. Why not a nation of observers of the social world that mirrors the Victorian study of the natural one? Why not "field" observers — individuals who keep an eye out for the telltale signs that announce the appearance of a new species, the small changes in patterns of speech, clothing, body language, assembly, attitude, outlook, music, reading, aesthetics? Why not "desk" observers — individuals who examine field reports from several sources, looking for the larger pattern. The Internet gives us a new technology that allows for acts of cooperation and contribution of which the Victorians could not dream. Why not a marriage of 19th-century passions and contemporary technologies?

Imperial passion

Obviously, our study of plenitude can't look *exactly* like the English one for several reasons. As Barber tells us, the English were keen on natural history because it was thought to be morally uplifting, a good source of exercise, and a fine excuse for gentlemen to shoot things. Also, there is no grounds to suppose that the plenitude of the 20th century could be ordered in the comprehensive, illuminating manner Linnaeus supplied. And this means in turn that there is no tidy set of categories to inform the field and desk observer.

Most important, natural species do not mind being studied and collected; social species almost always do. The study of 19th-century plenitude was a part of an imperial passion for control, containment, and possession that was so much the spirit of the age. None of this sits well in our case — not least because many of our new species are constructed precisely to take issue with, deliberately to defy and potentially undo, the culture of the mainstream.[278]

Old Glory

English motives in the study of 20th-century plenitude would be presumptuous, patronizing, and wrong. This is clear in Jonathan Raban's treatment of social life on the Mississippi (*Old Glory*) and again in Bill Bryson's study of the American Midwest (*Lost Continent*).[279] In both cases, the author exerts himself to find something risible about the people around him and would have us join him as he rolls his eyes in quiet horror at the patent absurdity of their behaviour. These studies play plenitude "for laughs." They give us caricature when what we want is something more like Audubon.[280] The attitudes of the 19th century will not serve us. This is, to reverse the polarity of Said's work, a simple case of Occidentalism, where Western societies are held up for self-serving mockery and precious little illumination.[281]

It is also true that the English model of scholarship will not work for our purposes. Many of the great constructions of the 19th century looked a little like a spider's web. Presiding at the centre was a grave scholar—the American anthropologist Lewis Henry Morgan (1818–1881), the English etymologist James Murray (1837–1915), the English biographer Leslie Stephen (1832–1904)—and around him were arrayed hundreds, sometimes thousands, of educated amateurs from whom contributions would be solicited for the great man to organize and find a system in. Thus did Morgan, Murray, and Stephen piece together *Systems of Consanguinity*, the *Oxford English Dictionary*, and the *Dictionary of National Biography*, respectively.[282]

The trouble with this model is that it insists too much on the authority of the scholar at the centre and gives too little credit (in the form of respect or acknowledgement) to the tributary amateurs. The decline of hierarchy and the rise of an unusually talented and passionate lay public that have done so much to encourage plenitude also establish hopeful conditions for its study. Morgan, Murray, and Stephen cannot supply a model for the collective study of our plenitude, but they demonstrate the possibility of such a thing.

The present practitioners of the art of studying plenitude leave something to be desired as well. Journalists, market researchers, designers, pollsters, politicians, retailers, and the entertainment industries all keep an "ear to the ground."[283] The problem here is often that Victorian depth of study or care of observation is nowhere to be found. Many are too quick to rush their insights to market to give us much assurance. And there is a "one-off" quality about the exercise. Once a new species has been splashed about the paper or paraded before the client, inquiry stops, attention wanders, curiosity moves elsewhere. If the Victorians were too dour, too hierarchical for our purposes, certain contemporary observers are surely too glib and too easily distracted. The study of plenitude deserves a richer body of motives and a deeper fund of curiosity.

One solution exists already in the form of the "FAQ." In this case an individual takes it upon him or herself to answer the most "frequently asked questions" asked by visitors to a Web site or by participants in a mailing list or newsgroup. This can result in detailed and interesting ethnographic documents. To take just two examples, Peter Wake has given us an excellent treatment of goths, as Stephen Martin has of skinheads.[284] And these FAQs can be interactive and cooperative in a way that the Victorian model was not, as Chris Hilker's FAQ on raves demonstrates.[285] There is no substitute for this kind of reporting. It establishes an important foundation of the study of the contemporary world. We need to encourage the spirit of the FAQ. We need more FAQs and FAQs that go deeper. We need them to address issues they now leave untouched. We need the spirit of FAQ to run right through the world of plenitude, so that we are preparing these documents even when not accommodating puzzled visitors to a Web page.

But the documentation of plenitude cannot come merely from the members of the communities in question. Clearly, this solves the moral problems ("by what right, for what purpose do you study me") and the indignation ones ("who are you to study me"). But it opens still other, graver ones that have bedeviled anthropology and literature as these have been challenged by the issues of identity politics and representation.[286] But the FAQ route threatens a solipsistic universe in which we can only know (or at least report on) what we know by immediate experience — a morality as wrong and as nutty as the empiricism it resembles.

perfect world

In a perfect world, one in which the university community embraced the study of contemporary culture instead, as it more often does, of resisting it, we would have university classes devoted to the constant surveillance of popular culture in the effort to be the first one to spot, classify, and illuminate a new social species. In a less perfect world, we would have at least a class of individuals who, in the manner of the shortwave radio enthusiast or amateur astronomer, undertake the lonely work of scanning the world for new voices, comparing notes and addresses with other listeners. We have something like this in the impressive accomplishment of Nathaniel Wice and Steven Daly who have almost single-handedly documented large patches of the contemporary world.[287]

We *do* have a world filled with those who are skilled and sophisticated in the study of plenitude. This includes an entire generation of

North Americans and Europeans who now, as we have noted, live in a state of professional exile. The old guard are not budging. Popular culture will enter the university curriculum "over their dead bodies," as it were. Can retirement happen soon enough?

In the meantime, we live in a state of wilful ignorance. Some years ago I had a startling conversation with a Toronto psychiatrist who described the details of one of his patients as if they were all the young man's invention and a peculiarly ghoulish cry for help. It was clear he had never heard of The Cure, Anne Rice, or a long-standing *Anne Rice* species called "goth." I recently took part in a New York City "think tank" in which a psychologist of some standing demonstrated that he did not know that there had been an "alternative" movement in the world of youth.

How, pray tell me, are you supposed to offer advice to patients (or students) without this knowledge? But there is a more compelling question. How does one spend hundreds, nay, thousands, of hours talking to patients (or students) and not end with a pretty handy knowledge of goths and the alternative movement? What, in the psychological case particularly, are you talking to them about? These species of social life are not merely the "idiom" in which larger psychological (and educational) issues work themselves out. They are the very language that gives these issues shape, and form, and force.

In sum, we have motive and we have means. We have precedent and personnel. We have urgency. What's lacking? Is it only the participation of a generation of intellectuals and gatekeepers who have declared popular culture and contemporary culture beneath their dignity or somehow beyond their intelligence? Please do not tell me that what stands between us and self-knowledge is merely the selfishness of a single generation. Must we wait until this generation (for whom popular culture remains an active but guilty pleasure) enters retirement before plenitude can have a profession of its own?

Conclusion

ALL THAT CAN BE IMAGINED must be. No genuine potentiality of being can remain unfulfilled. Plato's theory of the natural world applies to our social one. Heterogeneity shows itself everywhere. The body politic fizzes with innovation. The categories of gender split and multiply endlessly. The ancient "seven ages of man" are now in the process of squaring themselves. Terrifying creatures multiply at almost the pace that good ones do. Categories of time and life-style change over and over again. New ideas, models, and realities of the workplace and the family emerge constantly. We are busting out all over.

terrifying creatures

Plenitude is driven by many developments in the contemporary world. The eclipse of the authority of science, social science, religion, and polite society contributed mightily. The rise of a Romantic ideology, individualism, liberalism, relativism, new diffusion centres, new gatekeepers and influences, and new marketing, broadcasting, Internet, and journalism techniques — all these contributed as well. There are many good reasons why plenitude should have visited us with such conviction and power.

But we should not treat plenitude as the sum of these parts — the monarch's body of bodies. Let us treat it, as Plato would have done, as a force that exists *sui generis*, as an imperative unto itself. Where there is room for new possibilities, there we can expect to find them. The culture of commotion is driven to this diversity. It is driven by this diversity. Let us give this diversity its due. Let us look for it.

Snowstorms in Toronto are glorious events. In our neighbourhood, Riverdale, people who are housebound and all but invisible much of the winter suddenly appear en masse to shovel their walks. It is a blizzard of possibilities. Our street, Langley, fills with neighbours: Chinese, straights, culinary enthusiasts, Greeks, retired people, WASPs, union members, skaters, gays, professionals, African

snowstorms

Canadians, working class, white collar, occasional labourers, small business owners, and students. There is diversity within the diversity.

construction workers Some of the Chinese are from Hong Kong, some from Mainland China, some from families that have lived in Canada for four generations. There are many types of straights, many types of gays and lesbians. We have a rock star, an actor, a publisher, an account executive, the owner of a stationery store, lawyers, a locksmith, an instructor at a community college, construction workers, university students, and the unemployed. We have owners and renters living in single-family units, rooming houses, duplexes, and condos. There are many people who are not represented. We have no CEOs, goths, geeks, transgenderists, same-sex-parent families, Xtreme athletes, or fashion mavens. Not yet. Or possibly, they don't shovel their walks.

This plenitude raises questions. How can we live in a society that admits of this kind of diversity? Is there a danger that fellow feeling will simply end? Can we be reduced to little solipsistic pockets? Are we observing the end of commonality? How do we create commonality in the face of such difference? These are the political questions. The intellectual ones are equally numerous and equally pressing. How are we to think about heterogeneity of this order? Can we establish a comprehending global view? Is a global view still possible?

As we have seen, our record on plenitude has been something less than stellar. Genuinely illuminating political ideas or intellectual approaches are in short supply. I believe it is not until we deal with plenitude *as* plenitude that we can expect any relief on this score. For the moment, we can say only that we have made our world vastly more mystifying than it needs to be. A theory of plenitude is one opportunity to begin to move beyond these inclinations and see the structure in the chaos, the culture in the commotion.

From a cultural point of view, this is an urgent undertaking. For we know what our culture *generally* does with difference. It uses it as a point of fission, differentiation, provocation, and, sometimes, open hostility. If our world is filling up with differences, if it must fill with differences, we are in for a rather bad time of it; potentially a Northern Ireland for us all.

But if difference is being replaced by plenitude, a rather less intransigent creature, things are not quite so grim. According to this model, diversity becomes a thing of richness more than provocation, the occasion of curiosity more than antagonism. And so much the better. But if this *is* happening, hadn't we better say so and get on with the business of discovering what plenitude is and how it works? If we are entering a new Cambrian era and our social world is going to continue to explode with new and unprecedented species, surely it's time to stop insisting that the sky is falling.

Baudrillard treats us to a vision of the contemporary world that emphasizes its "inertia, exhaustion and endings." But what is truly astonishing about the culture of commotion is it robustness, generative ability, and endless stream of innovation. Plenitude is now in the process of transforming us. Monolithic categories are giving way to multiple ones. We have lost the tidy set of "shapes" that used to organize our world. Certainly, plenitude makes for a perplexing world. But it need not remain perplexing. Plato, for one, would have been completely unsurprised. Martians, probably, too. ✹

Culture by Commotion

Notes

1. Robert Potts, "An Adaptable Gather: The Revival of the Penguin Modern Poets Series," *Times Literary Supplement*, 7 July 1995, 31.

2. Henri Mendras with Alistair Cole, *Social Change in Modern France: Towards a Cultural Anthropology of the Fifth Republic* (Cambridge: Cambridge University Press, 1991), 207.

3. Yo Yo Ma, qtd. in Jamie James, "Yo-Yo Ma May Be a National Institution, but He Continues to Reinvent Himself," *New York Times*, 31 December 1995, H32.

4. Philip D. Morgan, general introduction to *Diversity and Unity in Early North America*, ed. Philip D. Morgan (London: Routledge, 1993), 1.

5. Dean MacCannell and Juliet Flower MacCannell, *The Time of the Sign: A Semiotic Interpretation of Modern Culture* (Bloomington: Indiana University Press, 1982), 7.

6. Fredric Jameson, "Postmodernism and Consumer Society," in *The Anti-Aesthetic: Essays on Postmodern Culture*, ed. Hal Foster (Port Townsend, WA: Bay Press, 1983), 114.

7. Ted Polhemus, *Street Style: From Sidewalk to Catwalk* (London: Thames and Hudson, 1994), 9.

8. Linda Hutcheon, *A Poetics of Postmodernism: History, Theory, Fiction* (London: Routledge, 1988), 7.

9. Tom Rowlands, qtd. in Jason Fine, "The Hardstuff: Are the Chemical Brothers Techno's First Rock Stars?" *Option* 72 (January–February 1997): 62.

10. Arthur Coleman Danto, *Beyond the Brillo Box: The Visual Arts in Post-Historical Perspective* (New York: Farrar, Straus, and Giroux, 1992), 225, 226.

11. Robert N. Bellah et al., eds., *Habits of the Heart: Individualism and Commitment in American Life* (Berkeley: University of California Press, 1985), 277.

12. Clifford Geertz, "Blurred Genres: The Refiguration of Social Thought," in *Local Knowledge: Further Essays in Interpretive Anthropology* (New York: Basic Books, 1983), 20, 21.

13. Kathy MacKenzie, public lecture, Toronto, Ontario, 16 January 1997.

14. Arlene W. Saxonhouse, *Fear of Diversity: The Birth of Political Science in Ancient Greek Thought* (Chicago: University of Chicago Press, 1992).

15. Diana Crane, *The Transformation of the Avant-Garde: The New York Art World, 1940–1985* (Chicago: University of Chicago Press, 1987), 40.

16. Diane Von Furstenberg, qtd. in Dana Wood, "Table-Hopping," *W.* 25, no. 11 (1996): 81.

17. Margo Jefferson, "Dennis Rodman, Bad Boy as Man of the Moment," *New York Times*, 30 January 1997, C13.

18. Kathy Silberger, "The Illbient Underground," *Option* 70 (September–October 1996): 61.

19. Tricky, "Christiansands," on *Pre-Millenium Tension*, Polygram, 1996.

20. Isaiah Berlin, "Alleged Relativism in Eighteenth-Century European Thought," in *The Crooked Timber of Humanity* (New York: Fontana Press, 1990), 90.

21. I lifted this quote from Chris Hilker's Web page http://www.hyperreal.com/raves/altraveFAQ.html. I have been unable to find its origin. Suggestions, please, to grant@cultureby.com.

22. Roseanne Arnold, *My Lives* (New York: Ballantine Books, 1994), xiii.

23. For more on Frank Black (nee Charles Thompson, a.k.a. Black Francis, lead singer of the Pixies), see http://www.cruzio.com/~drg/frank_black/contents.html, and especially the Pixies album *Bossanova*. See also Larry Kanter, "The Suburban Serenity of Frank Black," *Option* 69 (July–August 1996): 51. Frank Black is not the first musician to look to outer space. For some years, the German punk-reggae artist Nina Hagen has claimed to be an alien. P-Funk specialist George Clinton claims that black people descended from outer space (Mothership Connection!). For more on the theme in black music and literature (e.g., Sun Ra, Lee Perry, Greg Tate, Samuel Delaney), see the extraordinary documentary *The Last Angel of History* (1996), directed by John Akomfrah.

24. Robert Zubrin and Richard Wagner, *The Case for Mars: The Plan to Settle the Red Planet and Why We Must* (New York: The Free Press, 1997).

25. Voltaire thought Plato was mistaken—not because species were not numerous, but because there was, mysteriously, room for even more than Plato had imagined. P.B. Medawar and J.S. Medawar, *Aristotle to Zoos: A Philosophical Dictionary of Biology* (Cambridge, MA: Harvard University Press, 1983), 134.

26. Arthur O. Lovejoy, *The Great Chain of Being: A Study of the History of an Idea* (Cambridge, MA: Harvard University Press, 1950), 52.

27. Plato did not apply the notion of plenitude to the social world. He believed that this world was capable of relative homogeneity. It was left to his student, Aristotle, to consider plenitude in the social world. "Aristotle deals with observed diversity in the world, not through denial... but through typologies and hierarchy" (Arlene W. Saxonhouse, *Fear of Diversity: The Birth of Political Science in Ancient Greek Thought* [Chicago: University of Chicago Press, 1992], 191). As we shall see, Aristotle's strategies for comprehending the diversity of the social world no longer serve us. Arthur O. Lovejoy, *The Great Chain of Being: A Study of the History of an Idea* (Cambridge, MA: Harvard University Press, 1950), 58–59.

28. William Herbert Sheldon, *The Varieties of Human Physique: An Introduction to Constitutional Psychology* (New York: Hafner, 1963). Arnold Mitchell, *The Nine American Lifestyles: Who We Are and Where We're Going* (New York: Macmillan, 1983). The New Age version of the trend: "The Enneagram is an ancient teaching that describes the beliefs, thoughts, feelings, motivation and behavior of nine different

types of people" (Learning Annex brochure [Toronto], November–December 1996, 8). *pages 19—23*
Gail Sheehy, *New Passages: Mapping Your Life across Time* (New York: Random House, 1995). Michael Adams recently identified 12 "social values tribes" (*Sex in the Snow* [Toronto: Viking Canada, 1997]).

29. For another review, one I discovered only after the completion of this section, see Robert John Ackermann, *Heterogeneities: Race, Gender, Class, Nation, and State* (Amherst: University of Massachusetts Press, 1996).

30. See Peter Laslett, *A Fresh Map of Life: The Emergence of the Third Age* (London: Weidenfeld and Nicolson, 1989) for an account of old models of ageing and his theory of the "third age" of life in which individuals are "free to realize personal purposes" (152).

31. See for instance the Web site http://www.cyberzine.org/html/GLAIDS/Diversity/ Diversitypage.html, and especially the Senior Action in a Gay Environment (SAGE).

32. On this phenomenon, see Jennie Keith, *Old People as People: Social and Cultural Influences on Aging and Old Age* (Boston: Little, Brown, 1982) and Sharon R. Kaufman, *The Ageless Self: Sources of Meaning in Late Life* (Madison: University of Wisconsin Press, 1986). Fitzgerald is characteristically sensitive to the invention taking place in this age group (but surely wrong to argue that this was a group of whom "society had as yet no set of expectations and no vision" [20]!). See also Frances Fitzgerald, "Sun City" (1983), in *Cities on a Hill: A Journey through Contemporary American Cultures* (New York: Touchstone, Simon and Schuster, 1987). For the popular literature that picks up this theme, see Deepak Chopra, *Ageless Body, Timeless Mind* (New York: Harmony Books, 1993). I have used the term "selfhood" loosely here. This is of course one of the key notions to be investigated, not assumed, in this book, and I will return to the term and the topic below.

33. Florida Scott-Maxwell, *The Meaning of My Days* (New York: Alfred A. Knopf, 1973), 19.

34. For an exceptionally interesting ethnographic look at the movement away from orthodox categories, see Philip Weiss, "And at Their Age! The New In-My-70s Life Style," *The Age Boom*, special issue of *New York Times Magazine,* 9 March 1997, 63–65. The fact and the contents of this issue mark how much change is taking place here.

35. This research was done at the Institute of Contemporary Culture at the Royal Ontario Museum and it resulted in an exhibit there entitled *Toronto Teenagers: Coming of Age in the 1990s.*

36. *Family Ties* was a situation comedy that ran on NBC from September 1982 to September 1989. Unexpectedly, it proved to be an ideological beachhead of the neoconservative movement of the decade, converting teens to Reaganesque and Republican values. Alex Keaton (the 17 year old played by Michael J. Fox) slept with a picture of William F. Buckley over his bed. Designed as an object of mockery, this character surprised everyone by becoming a champion of the "preppie" era.

37. This tremendous speciation in the teen world has not been well documented. *Toronto Teenagers* documented five categories: punks, preps, heavy metal, b-boys/ girls, and hippies. Ted Polhemus documents the stylistic signatures of many more in *Street Style: From Sidewalk to Catwalk* (London: Thames and Hudson, 1994).

pages 23–24 38. From a white, middle-class, professional woman in her late 40s in Toronto, Ontario, October 1990.

39. Stuart Hall and Tony Jefferson, eds., *Resistance through Rituals: Youth Subcultures in Post-War Britain* (London: Hutchinson, 1976). For Dick Hebdige's characteristically brilliant account of skinheads, see "Hiding in the Light: Youth Surveillance and Display," in *Hiding in the Light: On Images and Things* (London: Routledge, 1988), 17–36. But notice this characteristic phrase: "When disaffected adolescents from the inner city, more particularly when disaffected, inner city unemployed adolescents resort to symbolic and actual violence, they are playing with the only power at their disposal: the power to discomfit. The power, that is, to pose — to pose a threat" (18). See also Paul Willis, *Learning to Labor: How Working Class Kids Get Working Class Jobs* (New York: Columbia University Press, 1981). I am not saying there is no resistance in the world of teens or that there is something wrong with seeing it in this light. I am saying merely this should not be designated our unvarying point of departure and arrival. See Sue Widdicombe and Robin Wooffitt, *The Language of Youth Subcultures: Social Identity in Action* (New York: Harvester Wheatsheaf, 1995), and John Davis, *Youth and the Condition of Britain: Images of Adolescent Conflict* (London: Athlone Press, 1990), 13–14, for other versions of this criticism.

40. As Marshall Sahlins cautions: theory that asks us to forget what we know must invite suspicion.

41. *This Is Spinal Tap*, 1984, dir. Rob Reiner. Metallica, once the preeminent heavy metal band, offered "Kill 'Em All" as their 1983 debut. For an interesting transactional account of this music, see Deena Weinstein, *Heavy Metal: A Cultural Sociology* (New York: Lexington Books, 1991). See also the very useful primer by Paul Elliott and Jon Hotton, *The Best of Metal: The Essential CD Guide* (San Francisco: Collins-Publishers, 1993).

42. The term "headbanging" comes from rockers themselves, and it is used to describe the once obligatory (and still popular) characteristic rocking motion of the head and upper body with which heavy metal fans kept time to the music (body as metronome). It can be observed in many heavy metal videos but is especially conspicuous in the video for the AC/DC song "Thunderstruck" (from the album *Razor's Edge*) where an amphitheatre of fans can be seen "handbanging" together. I use "tribal" here with the greatest discomfort for reasons that will become clear.

43. For more on b-boys and b-girls, see the section "Locating Hip Hop" in *Microphone Fiends: Youth Music and Youth Culture*, ed. Andrew Ross and Tricia Rose (New York: Routledge, 1994).

44. Peter Wake, "Goths: Frequently Asked Questions," http://www.cis.ohio-state.edu/hypertext/faq/usenet/gothic-faq/faq.html. This group bears a more than passing resemblance to the melancholic man. Anthony Esler, *The Aspiring Mind of the Elizabethan Younger Generation* (Durham, NC: Duke University Press, 1966). See also Anne Williams, *Art of Darkness: A Poetic of Gothic* (Chicago: University of Chicago Press, 1995), Nina Auerbach, *Our Vampires, Ourselves* (Chicago: University of Chicago Press, 1995), and T.J. Lexus Ainsbury, "An Interview with . . . ," *The Ethnographic Interview Series on*

Videotape, 3 February 1996. See the remarkable video work of Trent Reznor and his band Nine Inch Nails for a glimpse of the goth aesthetic and goth values. *pages 25–28*

45. I am indebted to several conversations in the early 1990s with a Toronto punk called "Chaz" with whom I have lost touch. (Chaz, phone home.) See also Kathryn Joan Fox, "Real Punks and Pretenders: The Social Organisation of a Counterculture," *Journal of Contemporary Ethnography* 16 (1987): 344–70, and Legs McNeil and Gillian McCain, *Please Kill Me: The Uncensored Oral History of Punk* (New York: Grove Press, 1996). My review leaves out the dance scene, for an exceedingly good account of which see Sarah Thorton, *Club Cultures: Music, Media and Subcultural Capital* (Hanover, NH: Wesleyan University Press, 1996).

46. Grant McCracken, "Clothing as Language: Requiem for a Metaphor," in *Culture and Consumption* (Bloomington: Indiana University Press, 1988), 57–70.

47. I do not want to go too far in the other direction. When I refuse the notion of pastiche, I do not want to give support to the camp who insist, quite stupidly in my opinion, on treating types as tribes. (See, for instance, Daniel Wojcik, *Punk and Neo-Tribal Body Art* [Jackson: University Press of Mississippi 1995], and Michel Maffesoli, *The Time of the Tribes: The Decline of Individualism in Mass Society* [London: Sage, 1996].)

48. Some feminists dispute the "natural, biologically determined" qualities assigned by our culture to the gender category "female," only to insist on "natural and biologically determined" qualities of their own. See Janice Raymond, *The Transsexual Empire: The Making of the She-Male* (Boston: Beacon Press, 1979).

49. Judith Butler, *Gender Trouble: Feminism and the Subversion of Identity* (London: Routledge, 1990). See also Marjorie Garber, *Vested Interest: Cross-Dressing and Cultural Anxiety* (New York: Routledge, 1992).

50. See Joanne Gottlieb and Wald Gayle, "Smells Like Teen Spirit: Riot Grrrls, Revolution and Women in Independent Rock," in *Microphone Fiends: Youth Music and Youth Culture*, ed. Andrew Ross and Tricia Rose (New York: Routledge, 1994), 250–74, for a particularly good treatment of the issue. They show early female rock stars imitated male music, and the "riot grrrl" phenomenon that created something new.

51. Ellen Fein and Sherrie Schneider, *The Rules: Time-Tested Ways for Capturing the Heart of Mr. Right* (New York: Warner Books, 1995). Some 50,000 copies of this book sold in September of 1996: "...*The Rules* is not just a book; it's a movement" (Elizabeth Gleich, "Playing Hard to Get," *Time* 48, no. 18 [1996], 57–58).

52. Women who follow this book call themselves Rules Girls and speak of "doing the Rules" on men: "Ellen Fein...did the Rules on her to-be husband and has been married to him for 10 years now" ("Sherrie Schneider Conference on *The Rules*," 22 February 1995, http://www.pathfinder.com/@@eNLOPQUAPM4k1pqn/twep/Library/Psychology_Self_Help/The_Rules1.html).

53. "New Men for Jesus," *Economist*, 3 June 1995, 21–22. It is estimated that over 500,000 American men attended weekend stadium rallies for the Promise Keepers movement in 1994.

54. The best case in point is Michael Kimmel, *Manhood in America: A Cultural History* (New York: The Free Press, 1995). See also Gail Bederman, *Manliness and*

Civilization (Chicago: University of Chicago Press, 1995); Rowena Chapman and Jonathan Rutherford, *Male Order: Unwrapping Masculinity* (London: Lawrence and Wishart, 1988); Terry A. Kupers, *Revisioning Men's Lives* (New York: Guilford Press, 1993); Victor J. Seidler, *Rediscovering Masculinity* (London: Routledge, 1989). This work has a historical dimension as well — see, for instance, Mark C. Carnes and Clyde Griffen, eds., *Meanings for Manhood: Construction of Masculinity in Victorian America* (Chicago: University of Chicago Press, 1990).

55. See, for instance, Herb Goldberg, *The Hazards of Being Male: Surviving the Myth of Masculine Privilege* (New York: New American Library, 1976).

56. Marvin Harris, *America Now: The Anthropology of a Changing Culture* (New York: Simon and Schuster, 1981), 100.

57. Esther Newton, *Mother Camp: Female Impersonators in America* (Chicago: University of Chicago Press, 1979), xii.

58. Frances Fitzgerald, "The Castro," in *Cities on a Hill: A Journey through Contemporary American Cultures* (New York: Touchstone, Simon and Schuster, 1987), 62–63.

59. Michel Foucault, *The History of Sexuality*, trans. Robert Hurley (New York: Vintage Books, 1980), 101. See also Earl Jackson, Jr., "Scandalous Subjects: Robert Gluck's Embodied Narratives," *differences* 3, no. 2 (1991): 112–34, especially p. 115.

60. See the "Queerskin" page at http://www.geocities.com/WestHollywood/4388/skin.html.

61. I am indebted to an excellent source: Gilbert Herdt, ed., *Gay Culture in America: Essays from the Field* (Boston: Beacon Press, 1992). See particularly E. Michael Gorman's "The Pursuit of the Wish: An Anthropological Perspective on Gay Male Subculture in Los Angeles" and Stephen O. Murray's "Components of Gay Community in San Francisco," both in Herdt, and Bill Stern, "We're Here, We're Queer, and We're Hungry: Gay Restaurants Out Themselves," *LA Weekly*, 15 April 1994. I am also indebted to conversations with Jim McKenna, Bill Stern, and Irmi Karl. My characterizations of these conversations are my own — and may or may not represent their opinions successfully.

62. Corey Y. Creekmur and Alexander Doty, eds., *Out in Culture: Gay, Lesbian and Queer Essays* (Durham, NC: Duke University Press, 1995). Leslie C. Smith, "Not So Strange Bedfellows," *Globe and Mail*, 9 January 1997, D1. Daniel Mendlesohn, "We're Here! We're Queer! Let's Get Coffee! Notes on the Mainstreaming of a Once-Edgy Subculture," *New York Magazine*, October 1996.

63. I understand that some readers are going to be annoyed at the "generalizing" and "stereotyping" that follows. In my own defence, to observe the plenitude in the lesbian community is surely one way to resist the more usual and more hostile stereotypes. More to the point, this points the way to a world in which one *cannot* generalize or stereotype about the lesbian community. It says this community is beginning to host the development of differences that will make stereotyping impossible (perhaps even generalizing as well.)

64. For this paragraph, I am indebted to the superlative work of Elizabeth Lapovsky Kennedy and Madeline D. Davis, *Boots of Leather, Slippers of Gold: The History of a Lesbian Community* (New York: Penguin Books, 1993), and an illuminating

ethnographic account in the first person by Leslie Feinberg, *Stone Butch Blues: A Novel* (Ithaca, NY: Firebrand Books, 1993).

65. Partly, this acknowledges Foucault's truth (that protest that uses mainstream categories helps to perpetuate them), and partly it is the exercise of a semiotic mischief that cannot be summoned for some purposes and contained for others.

66. Bianca Troll, "Bianca's Lesbian Lexicon," http://bianca.com/shack/, 1994. Troll describes this group as one that "typically embraces old style feminism, and is generally seen by younger, sex positive dykes as sexually uptight, too PC and lacking fashion sense."

67. My chief source is the exemplary Lindsy Van Gelder and Pamela Robin Brandt, *The Girls Next Door: Into the Heart of Lesbian America* (New York: Simon and Schuster, 1996). It is worth pointing out that the last category here is really little more than a holding category. The new category is filled with diversity, as lesbians in their teens and 20s adopt no single, identifying look and perspective, but prefer instead to seek out many different possibilities. In this case the very idea of a "lesbian" identity is itself exploded — just as the notion of a "straight" persona once was.

68. Van Gelder and Brandt offer an account of the Michigan's Womyn's Music Festival and the numerous and defining issues that constantly arose within it (Lindsy Van Gelder and Pamela Robin Brandt, *The Girls Next Door: Into the Heart of Lesbian America* [New York: Simon and Schuster, 1996], especially p. 74).

69. David Ehrenstein, "When It Comes to Sitcoms, Gays Rule," *Globe and Mail*, 12 October 1996, C4.

70. Van Gelder and Brandt observe the paradox that the lesbian community has been both less threatening to *and* more completely excluded from mainstream media — at least until 1993 when being a lesbian became suddenly more visible and more fashionable (Lindsy Van Gelder and Pamela Robin Brandt, *The Girls Next Door: Into the Heart of Lesbian America* [New York: Simon and Schuster, 1996], 21, 23, 31).

71. Vito Russo, *The Celluloid Closet: Homosexuality in the Movies*, rev. ed. (New York: Harper & Row, 1987). An episode of *Columbo* (featuring William Shatner and airing November 1995) showed two gay characters whose homosexuality was relatively incidental to the plot and may or may not satisfy Russo's condition.

72. David Ehrenstein, "When It Comes to Sitcoms, Gays Rule," *Globe and Mail*, 12 October 1996, C4.

73. There is more on this topic in the opening pages of book 2 in the Culture by Commotion series.

74. Bill Wyman, "Selling Out: Atlantic Records' New Target Market: Gay Music Fans," *Rolling Stone*, 16 November 1995, 40.

75. Gordene Olga MacKenzie, *Transgender Nation* (Bowling Green, OH: Bowling Green State University Popular Press, 1994), 62. MacKenzie disputes particularly the suggestion that most transgenderists feel themselves "trapped" in the wrong body (71–72).

76. Culled from "The Personals," *Village Voice*, 7 February 1995, 105–12.

77. Marjorie Garber, *Vested Interests: Cross-Dressing and Cultural Anxiety* (New York: Harper Perennial, 1992).

78. This reading seeks to move beyond the patronizing approach taken in the film

pages 33–34   *Paris Is Burning.* This documentary treats the transgenderist activity of a community of men in New York City as a desperate bid for a moment of stardom, as if these men were motivated only by a need to compensate for the status and other deprivations of their daily lives. This account would suit Thorstein Veblen, but much has happened in social scientific theory since the publication of his *The Theory of the Leisure Class* in 1912.

79. But this exercise is not always well received in feminist circles. Lisa Vogel, a founder of the Michigan Womyn's Music Collective, joined many festival participants in questioning whether transsexuals should be allowed to take part: "But those of us on the organizing end have a political and personal feeling of spirit that femaleness is not something that's particularly ambiguous — or created" (qtd. in Lindsy Van Gelder and Pamela Robin Brandt, *The Girls Next Door: Into the Heart of Lesbian America* [New York: Simon and Schuster, 1996], 76.

80. Kate Bornstein, *Gender Outlaw: On Men, Women and the Rest of Us* (New York: Routledge, 1994), 46–49. For the story of someone who underwent a female to male transformation, see Leslie Feinberg, *Stone Butch Blues: A Novel* (Ithaca, NY: Firebrand Books, 1993).

81. Culled from "The Personals," *Village Voice*, 7 February 1995, 105–12.

82. Don Steinberg, "Inside the Noisy World of Online Chat," *VirtualCity* 1, no. 2 (Winter 1996): 35–42. Steinberg reports *spivak* means "of indeterminate gender" and *neuter* "100 per cent gender-free."

83. I make this calculation by multiplying the first four categories by 8, the next two categories by 4 and the last two by 1.

84. Jean Baudrillard, *America*, trans. Chris Turner (London and New York: Verso, 1989), 47.

85. For a useful window on "RaiderNation," see http://www.raidernation.com. For Deadheads, see the superlative Nathaniel Wice and Steven Daly, "Deadheads," http://www.alt.culture.com/site/entries-text/deadheads.html, 1995. For Trekkies, there is so much on the Net, it's hard to know where to begin. See http://www.ica.net/pages/axl/startrek/startrek.html for a collection of links. For Hell's Angels, see Hunter S. Thompson, *Hell's Angels* (New York: Ballantine Books, 1967). For space-age bachelor-pad music or "LoungeNation," see http://www.chaoskitty.com/sabpm/sources.html. Mark Bofinger has begun the hard work of creating an Ulimate Frisbee theology. He defines "Frisbeetarianism" as "The belief that when you die, your soul goes up on the roof and gets stuck" (http://www.cs.uq.oz.au/personal/bof/Ultimate/intro.html). For Frisbee values illuminated by conflict, see http://www.mit.edu:8001/people/parinell/Testosterone Man1. For the *Rocky Horror Picture Show*, see http://chs-web.umdl.umich.edu/odd/RHPS/gfx/. For the Santa Cruz community of geeks, see http://samsara.circus.com:80/~omni/geek.html). Geeks define themselves as technically adept (as opposed to hackers who are "more programming intensive" and "nerds" who have no social skills) members of a literate, hyperinformed underground, and unified by the belief that "originality and strangeness are good."

86. Stephen Jay Gould, *Wonderful Life: The Burgess Shale and the Nature of History* (New York: W.W. Norton and Company, 1989).

87. T.S. Eliot, *The Sacred Wood: Essays on Poetry and Criticism*, 3d ed. (London: Methuen, 1932).

88. Grant McCracken, "Diderot Unities and the Diderot Effect," in *Culture and Consumption* (Bloomington: Indiana University Press, 1988), 121–23. There was a moment in the 80s when two life-styles actually looked like classes—preppies and Sloan Street Rangers—but in the end these came and went as all life-styles do (and as sociological verities, like class, mustn't ever).

89. I define life-styles as "Diderot unities": any constellation of attitudes, outlooks, behaviours, and stylistic identifiers in which the passion for some part of the world becomes the basis for a more general response to the world. This constellation may include or help influence fundamental values, voting, consumer and social behaviour. See Grant McCracken, "Diderot Unities and the Diderot Effect," in *Culture and Consumption* (Bloomington: Indiana University Press, 1988), 118–29.

90. See the intelligient Web essay "Dear Doc Marten: Questions and Answers about the Skinhead Subculture," by Stephen Martin, in which a distinction is drawn between skinheads and racist "boneheads." Martin asks us to remember "…the original Skinheads grew out of the melding of British working class youth, both white and black, with the music and fashions of the immigrant Jamaican community" (http://www.geocities.com/CapitolHill/Lobby/2231/ddm.html).

91. An "article of faith" from the Aryan Nation home page: "WE BELIEVE that the Cananite Jew is the natural enemy of our Aryan (White) Race. This is attested by scripture and all secular history. The Jew is like a destroying virus that attacks our racial body to destroy our Aryan culture and the purity of our Race" (http://stormfront.wat.com/stormfront/an.htm). See Stanley R. Barrett, *Is God a Racist? The Right Wing in Canada* (Toronto: University of Toronto Press, 1987).

92. Jeffrey Kaplan, *Radical Religion in America: Millenarian Movements from the Far Right to the Children of Noah* (Syracuse, NY: Syracuse University Press, 1997).

93. James Ridgeway, *Blood in the Face: The Ku Klux Klan, Aryan Nations, Nazi Skinheads, and the Rise of a New White Culture* (New York: Thunder's Mouth Press, 1990). The documentary film that accompanies this publication is very good and particularly recommended.

94. We will have a little more to say on how and why plenitude creates monsters in the section entitled "Plenitude's Fellow Travellers."

95. Mircea Eliade, *The Myth of the Eternal Return*, trans. Willard R. Trask (New York: Pantheon Books, 1954).

96. Ricardo J. Quinones, *The Renaissance Discovery of Time* (Cambridge: Harvard University Press, 1972). E.P. Thompson, "Time, Work-Discipline, and Industrial Capitalism," *Past and Present* 38 (December 1967): 56–97. Matei Calinescu, *Five Faces of Modernity* (Durham, NC: Duke University Press, 1987). Grant McCracken, "Time Comes Calling: A Reflection on Tatsuo Miyajima's Time House," *Tatsuo Miyajima: Time House,* ed. Marnie Fleming (Oakville, ON: Oakville Galleries, 1996).

97. Claude Levi-Strauss, *The Savage Mind* (Chicago: University of Chicago Press, 1966).

98. There is an extended discussion of the cultural significance of modernism in book 3 of this series.

99. David Halberstam, *The Fifties* (New York: Villard Books, 1993). Thomas Hine, *Populuxe* (New York: Alfred A. Knopf, 1986). Richard Horn, *Fifties Style: Then and Now* (Harmondsworth: Penguin, 1985). Julian Marias, *America in the Fifties and Sixties*, trans. Blanche De Puy and Harold C. Raley (University Park: Pennsylvania State University Press, 1972).

100. Todd Gitlin, *The Sixties: Years of Hope, Days of Rage* (New York: Bantam Books, 1987).

101. There is no definitive study of the 80s, but one of the most telling ethnographic documents of the decade is the movie *Metropolitan* (1990) directed by Whit Stillman. For a nice, if belated, repudiation of the 80s style, see Christopher Mason, "Hating the 80s: From Swags and Furbelows to Tea-Steeped Chintzes, the Trappings of an Ostentatious Era Still Haunt Us," *New York Times Magazine*, 13 April 1997, part 2: 22, 60.

102. Todd Gitlin, *The Sixties: Years of Hope, Days of Rage* (New York: Bantam Books, 1987), 209.

103. Robert Potts, "An Adaptable Gather: The Revival of the Penguin Modern Poets Series," *Times Literary Supplement*, 7 July 1995, 31.

104. Philip D. Morgan, general introduction to *Diversity and Unity in Early North America*, ed. Morgan (London: Routledge, 1993), 1.

105. Grant McCracken, *Big Hair* (New York: Overlook Press, 1996).

106. Ted Polhemus, *Street Style: From Sidewalk to Catwalk* (London: Thames and Hudson, 1994), 9.

107. Arthur Coleman Danto, *Beyond the Brillo Box: The Visual Arts in Post-Historical Perspective* (New York: Farrar, Straus and Giroux, 1992), 225, 226.

108. Neil Strauss, "Forget Pearl Jam. Alternative Rock Lives," *New York Times*, 2 March 1997, H34.

109. See the "official alt.rav FAQ" at http://www.hyperreal.com/raves/altraveFAQ.htm and the highly regarded "The Ecstatic Cybernetic Amino Acid Test" at http://www.hyperreal.com/raves/media/press/image.gz.

110. I am indebted to Dave Dyment for his instruction in contemporary music and for some of the details of this paragraph.

111. See the review by Chris Norris in *Spin* (http://www.rain.org/~truck/beck/written/spinode.html) and the Mark Kemp review in *Rolling Stone* (http://www.rain.org/~truck/ beck/written/rollode.html).

112. Jamie James, "Yo-Yo Ma May Be a National Institution, but He Continues to Reinvent Himself," *New York Times*, 31 December 1995, H32.

113. Fredric Jameson, "Postmodernism and Consumer Society," in *The Anti-Aesthetic: Essays on Postmodern Culture*, ed. Hal Foster (Port Townsend, WA: Bay Press, 1983), 114.

114. Linda Hutcheon, *A Poetics of Postmodernism: History, Theory, Fiction* (London: Routledge, 1988), 7.

115. Clifford Geertz, "Blurred Genres: The Refiguration of Social Thought," in

Books, 1983), 20, 21.

116. Henri Mendras with Alistair Cole, *Social Change in Modern France: Towards a Cultural Anthropology of the Fifth Republic* (Cambridge: Cambridge University Press, 1991), 207.

117. Dean MacCannell and Juliet Flower MacCannell, *The Time of the Sign: A Semiotic Interpretation of Modern Culture* (Bloomington: Indiana University Press, 1982), 7.

118. Tom Rowlands, qtd. in Jason Fine, "The Hardstuff: Are the Chemical Brothers Techno's First Rock Stars?" *Option* 72 (January–February 1997): 62.

119. Arlene W. Saxonhouse, *Fear of Diversity: The Birth of Political Science in Ancient Greek Thought* (Chicago: University of Chicago Press, 1992), 203.

120. Kathy Silberger, "The Illbient Underground," *Option* 70 (September–October 1996): 61.

121. Isaiah Berlin, "Alleged Relativism in Eighteenth-Century European Thought," in *The Crooked Timber of Humanity* (New York: Fontana Press, 1990), 90.

122. Stephen Jay Gould, *Wonderful Life: The Burgess Shale and the Nature of History* (New York: W.W. Norton and Company, 1989).

123. Edmund Sears Morgan, *The Puritan Family: Religion and Domestic Relations in Seventeenth-Century New England*, new ed. (New York: Harper & Row, 1966).

124. There will be more on this in book 2, where we will talk about Madonna in some detail.

125. Cynthia Rutherford, "Commitment and Other Fading Customs," *Globe and Mail*, 1 November 1995, A20.

126. The notion of "serial monogamy" introduced only a few years ago in the academic literature now circulates freely as a shared understanding of the incidence of divorce and remarriage. See also Robert S. Weiss, "A New Marital Form: The Marriage of Uncertain Duration," in *On the Making of Americans: Essays in Honor of David Riesman*, ed. Herbert J. Gans, Nathan Glazer, Joseph R. Gusfield, and Christopher Jencks (Philadelphia: University of Pennsylvania Press, 1979), 221–33.

127. Judith Stacey, *Brave New Families* (New York: Basic Books, 1990).

128. Ours is a society that creates many of its structures by seizing on particular events. See, for instance, Joseph R. Gusfield, "The Sociological Reality of America," in *On the Making of Americans: Essays in Honor of David Riesman*, ed. Herbert J. Gans, Nathan Glazer, Joseph R. Gusfield, and Christopher Jencks (Philadelphia: University of Pennsylvania Press, 1979), 41–62. The more traditional pattern is to make events conform to structure — even when this structure has a certain plasticity. For more on this discussion, see Marshall David Sahlins, *How "Natives" Think: About Captain Cook, for Example* (Chicago: University of Chicago Press, 1995), 247.

129. Christopher Lasch, *Haven in a Heartless World: The Family Besieged* (New York: Basic Books, 1977). This work disappoints for several reasons but mostly because it fails to see that some developments within and without the family are in fact new structures, not imperfections. Lasch consistently treats individualism and its consequences as a failure of moral and social standards. We have been capable of better

pages 52–56 than this since Durkheim. See Steven Lukes, *Emile Durkheim, His Life and Work: A Historical and Critical Study* (Harmondsworth: Penguin, 1973), 199.

130. A middle-class Canadian mother told me recently (spring 1996) of a new eating pattern for her 14-year-old daughter and friends. When shopping on Queen Street in Toronto, they buy their food separately and eat it together. This departs from one of the meta-pragmatic functions of the meal according to which the meal creates commonality by demanding commonality. In the cultural logic of this ritual moment: "We are the same thing (for this social moment) because we eat the same thing." I use the term "meta-pragmatic function" as it appears in Michael Silverstein, "Shifters, Linguistic Categories, and Cultural Description," in *Meaning in Anthropology*, ed. Keith H. Basso and Henry A. Selby (Albuquerque: University of New Mexico Press, 1976), 11–55.

131. Harold Bloom, *The Western Canon: The Books and School of the Ages* (New York: Harcourt Brace, 1994). Henry Louis Gates, Jr., *Loose Canons: Notes on the Culture Wars* (New York: Oxford University Press, 1992).

132. Joseph Tussman, *Experiment at Berkeley* (New York: Oxford University Press, 1969). For what it's worth, I am one of the children of this program, having taken the "Arts One" program at the University of British Columbia.

133. These are of course merely the opening principles of the status system. For the whole system in all of its glorious patterned complexity, see Georg Simmel, "Fashion," *International Quarterly* 10 (1904): 130–55. For my own effort to wrestle with this topic, see Grant McCracken, "Consumer Goods, Gender Construction, and a Rehabilitated Trickle-Down Theory," in Grant McCracken, *Culture and Consumption* (Bloomington: Indiana University Press, 1988), 93–103.

134. Sir Thomas Elyot, *The Boke Named the Governour* (1531; London: J.M. Dent, 1907); emphasis added.

135. Edward A. Shils, "Deference," in *The Logic of Social Hierarchies*, ed. Edward O. Laumann, Paul M. Siegel, and Robert W. Hodge (Chicago: Markham Publishing Company, 1970), 420–48.

136. Frances Trollope, *Domestic Manners of the Americans*, ed. Donald Smalley (1832; Gloucester, MA: 1974), 241–43.

137. The best treatment of this status system is Richard L. Bushman's magnificent recent work *The Refinement of America* (New York: Vintage, 1993). See also Karin Calvert, "The Function of Fashion in Eighteenth-Century America," in *Of Consuming Interests: The Style of Life in the Eighteenth Century*, ed. Cary Carson, Ronald Hoffman, and Peter J. Albert (Charlottesville: University Press of Virginia, 1994), 252–83; Jack P. Greene, "Convergence: Development of an American Society, 1720–1780," in *Diversity and Unity in Early North America*, ed. Philip D. Morgan (London: Routledge, 1993), 43–72; and Gertrude Himmelfarb, *The De-moralization of Society* (New York: Alfred A. Knopf, 1995).

138. There is, of course, a lively debate on whether and how far the values of superordinate families penetrated middle-class and working-class families. Roberts, for instance, finds evidence of influence; Cohen does not. See Elizabeth Roberts, *A Woman's Place: An Oral History of Working-Class Women, 1890–1940* (Oxford: Oxford Uni-

versity Press, 1984), and Lizabeth A. Cohen, "Embellishing a Life of Labor: An Inter-pretation of the Material Culture of American Working-Class Homes, 1885–1915," in *Material Culture Studies in America*, ed. Thomas J. Schlereth (Nashville: American Association for State and Local History, 1982), 222–36.

139. "Parlors were made for genteel performance, in imitation of aristocratic draw-ing rooms. They were tokens of the family's covenant with gentility, their claim on the dignity of a higher level of existence..." (Richard L. Bushman, *The Refinement of America: Persons, Houses, Cities* [New York: Vintage, 1993], xvi).

140. Peter York, *Style Wars and Other Options for Human Behavior* (London: Sidgwick and Jackson, 1980).

141. Diane Von Furstenberg, qtd. in Dana Wood, "Table-Hopping," W. 25, no. 11 (1996): 81.

142. Notice how the "up and down" imagery lingers on. Hierarchy may be dead (or dying) but it still supplies some of the most powerful metaphors for the social order. For more on trickle-up diffusion, see George A. Field, "The Status Float Phe-nomenon: The Upward Diffusion of Innovation," *Business Horizons* 13, no. 4 (August 1970): 45–52; Paul Blumberg, "The Decline and Fall of the Status Symbol: Some Thoughts on Status in a Post-Industrial Society," *Social Problems* 21, no. 4 (April 1974): 480–98; and Tom Wolfe, *Radical Chic and Mau-Mauing the Flak Catchers* (New York: Farrar, Straus and Giroux, 1970).

143. I use "operator" as it appears in James A. Boon, "Further Operations of Cul-ture in Anthropology: A Synthesis of and for Debate," in *The Idea of Culture in the Social Sciences*, ed. Louis Schneider and Charles Bonjean (Cambridge: Cambridge Uni-versity Press, 1973), 1–32.

144. In North America, only the Beatles have sold more. *The New Music*, CITY-TV, broadcast 10 August 1996.

145. Todd Gitlin, *The Sixties: Years of Hope, Days of Rage* (New York: Bantam Books, 1987).

146. Claudia B. Kidwell and Margaret C. Christman, *Suiting Everyone: The Democratization of Clothing in America* (Washington: Smithsonian Press, 1974).

147. Grant McCracken, "Ever Dearer in Our Thoughts: Patina and the Represen-tation of Status before and after the 18th Century," in Grant McCracken, *Culture and Consumption* (Bloomington: Indiana University Press, 1988), 31–43. For a treatment of the failure to fashion a traditional social hierarchy in the American context, see Robert H. Wiebe, *Self-Rule: A Cultural History of American Democracy* (Chicago: University of Chicago Press, 1995), 139–41.

148. Lionel Trilling, *Sincerity and Authenticity* (Cambridge: Harvard University Press, 1971).

149. Clyde Kluckhohn and Florence R. Kluckhohn, "American Culture: General-ized Orientations and Class Patterns," in *Conflicts of Power in Modern Culture*, ed. Lyman Louis, Finkelstein Bryson, and R.M. Maciver (New York: Cooper Square Pub-lishers, 1964), 111. Tim Onosko, *Wasn't the Future Wonderful? A View of Trends and Technology from the 1930s* (New York: E.P. Dutton, 1979). John Arthur Passmore,

pages 61–63 The Perfectibility of Man (New York: Charles Scribner's Sons, 1970). For a wonderful treatment of the participation of Walt Disney in the American cult of the future, see Seth Schiesel, "New Disney Vision Making the Future a Thing of the Past," *New York Times*, 23 February 1997, 1, 24.

150. Ron Rosenbaum, "Among the Believers," *New York Times Magazine*, 24 September 1995, 50–57, 62–64. On a visit to Tower Records in Toronto (June 1996), I was struck by the labels in the book section, which I reproduce here in their entirety: mayhem, outlaws, cyber, alternative, herbalism, aliens, spiritual, science fiction, religion, occult, horror, fantasy, gay/lesbian, sex nonfiction, sex fiction, drugs, body art, murder.

151. In the late 1980s, the medical community estimated that one in four Americans were visiting "quacks" and that the nation would spend $25 billion dollars on "quackery" in a single year. Indignation is directed especially towards iridology ("Quackery," *Mayo Clinic Health Letter*, June 1988, 1–8).

152. Gordene Olga MacKenzie, *Transgender Nation* (Bowling Green, OH: Bowling Green State University Popular Press, 1994), 2.

153. Bryan Wilson, "Historical Lessons in the Study of Sects and Cultures," in *Religion and the Social Order*, ed. David G. Bromley and Jeffrey K. Hadden, vol. 3 (Greenwich, CT: JAI Press, 1993), 66.

154. Melanie McGrath, *Motel Nirvana: Dreaming of the New Age in the American Desert* (New York: HarperCollins, 1995). Fred M. Frohock, *Healing Powers: Alternative Medicine, Spiritual Communities, and the State* (Chicago: University of Chicago Press, 1992). We may treat the growing popularity of magazines like *Fortean Times: The Journal of Strange Phenomena* as another indication in this shift in standards of credulity. *Fortean Times* has a lively sense of irony, and it suggests the new credulity has for some users a carefully crafted double logic: "Hey, this could be true" and "Hey, imagine anyone believing this is true."

155. "Cults of All Descriptions Proliferate across the U.S.," *Globe and Mail*, 4 April 1997, A2.

156. The *X-Files* "stigmata" episode (originally broadcast December 1996) shows this new pattern to perfection. In the face of evidence of stigmata, Mulder, normally quick to accept the unorthodox, remains doubtful. Scully, normally a sceptic, is a believer. Scully is the old model of belief. Mulder, the new.

157. See Mark Kingwell's recent book for a more systematic treatment of the new credulities. Kingwell convincingly treats this as the product of an end-of-century anxiety. I would argue that it also represents a deeper, more enduring cultural development that will survive into and expand to fill the 21st century. Mark Kingwell, *Dreams of Millennium: Report from a Culture on the Brink* (Toronto: Viking, 1996). See http://www.disinfo.com for a review of credulity on the Net.

158. Mark Leiren-Young, "X-treme Possibilities," *Shift* 4, no. 2 (1995): 18–22.

159. David Barboza, "Museum Provides the Plots, No Answer," *New York Times*, 28 May 1995, 14. Still more astonishing, some substantial part of the black community in the U.S. is prepared to entertain the possibility that the AIDS virus was created

by the American government to be used against them in a campaign of genocide. See Paul Raeburn, "One-Third of Blacks in Survey View AIDS as a Tool of Genocide," *Chicago Sun-Times*, 2 November 1995, 21. Raeburn points out that another third of the sample believed that the genocide theory was *possible*, leaving only one third of the sample who doubted it outright.

160. The "follow the money" phrase is from Oliver Stone's great conspiracy treatise, *JFK*. This phrase takes its pragmatic force (to bring the viewer in on the conspiracy to believe in conspiracies) by implying that those who would have profited from an event must necessarily be its authors.

161. For an excellent treatment, see Anthony Sampson, *Company Man: The Rise and Fall of Corporate Life* (New York: Random House, 1995), especially ch. 6, "The Airless Cage." The more classic statement is William H. Whyte, Jr., *The Organization Man* (New York: Simon and Schuster, 1956).

162. David Dorsey, *The Force* (New York: Random House, 1994). Arlie Russell Hochschild, *The Managed Heart: Commercialization of Human Feeling* (Berkeley: University of California Press, 1983). Richard M. Huber, *The American Idea of Success* (New York: McGraw-Hill Book Company, 1971).

163. Daniel Bell, *The Cultural Contradictions of Capitalism* (New York: Basic Books, 1976).

164. The great exception here is the extraordinary demands the corporation makes of the personal time of the individual, preempting, as it were, the very possibility of some kinds of personal development and transformation. This is well captured in Ron Howard's 1994 film *The Paper*. For the development of a new corporate model that demands more spontaneity, see Gary Hamel and C.K. Prahalad, *Competing for the Future* (Boston: Harvard Business School Press, 1994); Charles Handy, *The Age of Unreason* (London: Arrow Books, 1989); and Michael Hammer and James Champy, *Reengineering the Corporation* (New York: HarperBusiness, 1993).

165. I take the term "McJob" to refer to any job that is so routine as to be careless of the full creative ability of the individual occupying it. It may have originated in Douglas Coupland, *Generation X: Tales for an Accelerated Culture* (New York: St. Martin's Press, 1991). See also Warren Clements, "Many a Mc'll Make a Muckle," *Globe and Mail*, 10 August 1996, D6.

166. It has been widely observed (I do not know to whom I owe a footnote) that the race of black athletes is often modified and sometimes revised when they become especially accomplished. In the literal form of the revision, this is a genetic matter. After his World Series heroics, Reggie Jackson was discovered to have Latin ancestry. As Mohamed Ali became more famous, he was discovered to have Irish ancestry. The golf sensation Tiger Woods is now having his Thai heritage emphasized. In the more general form, race is virtually forgotten. Louis Armstrong, for instance, was no longer black, he was, well, famous. For a moment the same could be said for O.J. Simpson. This is of course before his infamy—whereupon he become black again. (Recall the famous *Time Magazine* cover in which his face was darkened.) Thus does racism protect itself against the possibility of refutation. There is an important exception here

and it may be a harbinger of things to come. Michael Jordan's blackness has not been revised as his celebrity established itself.

167. Cameron Crowe, qtd. in Bernard Weinraub, "Hollywood Learns Small Is Beautiful," *Globe and Mail*, 25 February 1997, D3. (Originally published in the *New York Times.*)

168. Mark Crispin Miller, "The Crushing Power of Big Publishing," *Nation*, 17 March 1997, 11–12.

169. Grant McCracken, "Culture and culture at the Royal Ontario Museum: A Ghost Story." Working paper.

170. Jules Henry, *Culture Against Man* (New York: Vintage, 1963). Dwight Macdonald, *Against the American Grain* (London: Gollancz, 1963). Daniel J. Boorstin, *The Americans: The Democratic Experience* (New York: Random House, 1973). Stuart Ewen, *Captains of Consciousness: Advertising and the Social Roots of the Consumer Culture* (New York: McGraw-Hill, 1976). Deborah Root, *Cannibal Culture: Art, Appropriation, and the Commodification of Difference* (Boulder, CO: Westview Press, 1996).

171. Jason Fine, "The Hardstuff: Are the Chemical Brothers Techno's First Rock Stars?" *Option* 72 (January–February 1997), 60–65. Fine is the editor of *Option*. His conversion on this issue is an exceedingly important "leading indicator" of the future of rock and roll. The new generation of women in rock are sampling. Sometimes this is unsurprising. Given their roots, Luscious Jackson might be *expected* to sample. But it is true even for those who come from a folkier, less electronic tradition (e.g., Ani DiFranco, Sarah McLachlan). I believe Lisa Germano is alone in having sampled her cat.

172. It is of course this sampling tradition that most encourages the postmodernists to suppose that contemporary culture is the site of empty signs in ceaseless circulation. The reader will tire perhaps when I mount my hobbyhorse once more, but this needs to be said: these signs are not empty. As a result of sampling, they carry very particular culture meanings from their origin to a new home.

173. I am grateful to Glouberman's work on this question. Most of the resources on which I draw come from his page: http://www.muchmusic.com/muchmusic/cyberfax/trademark.html.

174. http://www.rru.com/tru/#synopsis.

175. For a particularly good treatment of the cultural implications of copyright, see Jane Gaines, *Contested Culture: The Image, the Voice, and the Law* (Chapel Hill: University of North Carolina Press, 1991).

176. http://www.speakeasy.org/~dbrick/Melrose/stupid.html.

177. http://www.snpp.com/fox_letter.html.

178. I have this from a casual conversation with a Disney executive who will remain nameless here. This entire criticism could just as easily be brought against Warner Brothers.

179. On passivity as a condition of the Disney experience, see Alan Bryman, *Disney and His Worlds* (London: Routledge, 1995).

180. Ernest Troeltsch, *The Social Teaching of the Christian Churches*, trans. Olive Wyon, vol. 2 (New York: Harper Torchbooks, 1931), 514, 699, 702.

181. Robert A. Nisbet, *Social Change and History: Aspects of the Western Theory of Development* (New York: Oxford University Press, 1969), 51. Richard Handler and Jocelyn Linnekin, "Tradition, Genuine or Spurious," *Journal of American Folklore* 97, no. 385 (1984): 273–90. Wayne C. Booth, "Renewing the Medium of Renewal," in *Innovation/Renovation: New Perspectives on the Humanities*, ed. Ihab Hassan and Sally Hassan (Madison: University of Wisconsin Press, 1983), 133.

182. Gerald N. Izenberg, *Impossible Individuality: Romanticism, Revolution, and the Origins of Modern Selfhood, 1787–1802* (Princeton: Princeton University Press, 1992), 13. Izenberg's book argues that innovative individualism is only one half of the Romantic impulse.

183. For the best of these accounts, see Bernice Martin, *A Sociology of Contemporary Cultural Change* (Oxford: Basil Blackwell, 1981).

184. Charles Taylor, *Sources of the Self: The Making of the Modern Identity* (Cambridge: Harvard University Press, 1989), 376.

185. D.H. Lawrence, qtd. in John Carey, *The Intellectuals and the Masses: Pride and Prejudice among the Literary Intelligentsia, 1880–1939* (London: Faber and Faber, 1992), 77.

186. Edward Shils, "Mass Society and Its Culture" (1959), in *Mass Media in Modern Society*, ed. Norman Jacobs (New Brunswick: Transaction Publishers, 1992), 65.

187. Marshall Berman, *The Politics of Authenticity: Radical Individualism and the Emergence of Modern Society* (New York: Atheneum, 1980). Robert R. Ehman, *The Authentic Self* (Buffalo, NY: Prometheus Books, 1994). Fighting one's way to the authentic self is of course one of the great themes of Hollywood films.

188. Isaiah Berlin, *Four Essays on Liberty* (Oxford: Oxford University Press, 1969), 176–77.

189. Allan Bloom, *The Closing of the American Mind* (New York: Simon and Schuster, 1987), 25.

190. Howard Becker, *Outsiders: Studies in the Sociology of Deviance* (Englewood Cliffs, NJ: Prentice-Hall, 1963). Erving Goffman, *Stigma: Notes on the Management of Spoiled Identities* (Englewood Cliffs, NJ: Prentice-Hall, 1963). Foucault took up this academic enterprise with still more spectacular effects in *The History of Sexuality*.

191. I can hear a chorus of doubts here. Surely, someone will say, recent political developments on both the left and right in the U.S. suggest a certain closing down of tolerance.

192. Edward Shils, "Center and Periphery," in *Essays in Macrosociology* (Chicago: University of Chicago Press, 1975). For the way this relationship worked in the world of fashion, see Peter York, *Modern Times* (London: Heinemann, 1984), 10. For a sense of how it worked in the world of art, see Diana Crane, *The Transformation of the Avant-Garde: The New York Art World, 1940–1985* (Chicago: University of Chicago Press, 1987).

193. "[T]he time when fashion came from Europe, and American designers were dismissed as either second-rate stylists or rip-off artists—who deliberately showed their collections after Paris and Milan so that they could 'adapt' the latest ideas from Europe

Culture by Commotion

— is, mercifully, past" (Anna Wintour, letter from the editor, *Vogue*, September 1996, 38).

194. Robert E. Park, *Human Communities* (Glencoe, IL: The Free Press, 1952), 86. Park, a journalist turned social scientist, was an intelligent observer of this phenomenon.

195. Russell Lynes, *The Taste Makers: The Shaping of American Popular Taste* (New York: Dover Publications, 1980).

196. Richard Linklater helped to define the "twenty something" generation with his film *Slacker*. Rush Limbaugh helped to define a conservative philosophy and a movement with his radio program. Tom Wolfe helped define the 80s with *The Right Stuff* and undo it with *The Bonfire of the Vanities*. Werner Erhard created the EST movement, and Ben and Jerry helped to redefine the notion of corporate responsibility. Vivian Westwood helped to define the punk movement and several subsequent aesthetics/species with her contributions to fashion. Joyce Meyer is in the process of changing the nature of TV evangelism. Susan Powter offered a new model of weight control (Susan Powter, *Stop the Insanity: Eat, Breathe, Move and Change the Way You Look and Feel—Forever* [New York: Simon and Schuster, 1993]).

197. The best example of this diffusion pattern known to me is the design work of Tinker Hatfield for Nike.

198. Donald Katz, *Just Do It: The Nike Spirit in the Corporate World* (New York: Random House, 1994), 64–65. See Marshall Sahlins on the market's ability to help create new categories of person. Marshall Sahlins, *Culture and Practical Reason* (Chicago: University of Chicago Press, 1976).

199. Steven L. Goldman, Roger N. Nagel, and Kenneth Preiss, "Why Seiko Has 3,000 Watch Styles," *New York Times*, 9 October 1994, F9.

200. Steven Marshall's Channel Zero is perhaps the best case in point.

201. Steven Levy, "How the Propeller Heads Stole the Electronic Future," *New York Times Magazine*, 24 September 1995, 58–59.

202. Tom Wolfe, *Radical Chic and Mau-Mauing the Flak Catchers* (New York: Farrar, Straus and Giroux, 1970); Hunter S. Thompson, *Hell's Angels* (New York: Ballantine Books, 1967); Peter York, *Style Wars and Other Options for Human Behavior* (London: Sidgwick and Jackson, 1980); *Wired*, September 1994; *Paper*, November 1994; Jerry Adler, "The Rise of the Overclass," *Newsweek*, 31 July 1995, 33–46.

203. Gordene Olga MacKenzie, *Transgender Nation* (Bowling Green, OH: Bowling Green State University Popular Press, 1994), 6.

204. See Diana Crane, *The Transformation of the Avant-Garde: The New York Art World, 1940–1985* (Chicago: University of Chicago Press, 1987), 40, for an account of this change in the world of art. A recognition of this factor has entered even our vision of the future. The modernist "future," the one that prevailed in the postwar period through the 1960s, always showed the world to come as a place that was shiny with novelty. Everything would be redesigned, nothing would survive the purge of the new. Sometime in the 1970s we began, in popular culture, to entertain a different future, a composted future, in which things lived on often in a state of disarray. Thus spoke *Blade Runner* and the *Star Wars* trilogy. This has been intensified by those who now expect the future to look like Tarantino's vision of the 1960s, as a place were pop-

ular culture returns over and over again and the Zippo lighter remains forever in style.

205. As Eric Stoltz's character in *Pulp Fiction* (1994) put it, "Coke is dead as … dead; heroin is coming in in a big fucking way." There is no doubt that heroin's present popularity has something to do with its excluded status and street credibility. For a generation whose sensibility has been crafted by Quentin Tarantino and Douglas Coupland, many drugs now seem preposterously sunny and naïve. *Trainspotting* claimed to be anti-drug but helped to create a certain "heroin chic." For a glimpse of one life on the nod, see Mike Sager, "Generation H," *GQ* 65, no. 9 (1995), 276–83, 303, 306. Also see the excellent article by George Kalogerakis, "Stoned Again: Americans in Large Numbers Are Not Saying No to Marijuana, Psychedelics and Even Heroin," *New York*, 1 May 1995, 41–47.

206. For an excellent account of the "nothing to lose" Mexican boyhood of former featherweight champion Jorge Maromero Paez, see Marc Gerald, "The Tumbler," http://www.word.com/machine/thetumbler, 1996.

207. The cyberpunk, noir science fiction novelists (e.g., William Gibson and the lesser Bruce Sterling) have made a positive fetish of this high-risk proposition. They are persuaded that the societies of the future will consist of two groups: the hugely conformist who work for multinational corporations and all the rest who eke out an existence in the tippy netherworld of eccentricity and computer-aided rebellion. See *Tank Girl* for one of the latest appearances of this peculiar idea. What is odd about this idea is how little it comes to terms with the ideas of plenitude and transformation. Individuals on both sides of this political divide are fixed into unchanging roles and lives.

208. I owe this observation to Lawrence W. Levine, *Highbrow/Lowbrow: The Emergence of Cultural Hierarchy in America* (Cambridge: Harvard University Press, 1988), 171–72.

209. The "multiplication of everything" is from Henry James, *The American Scene*, annotation by Leon Edel (Bloomington: Indiana University Press, 1968), 131. For James's horror of the "inconceivable alien" of Ellis Island, see p. 85. But we should not overlook the complexity and the sheer power of James's curiosity for he also speaks of the "continuity," the "affinity," the "queer sauce" that manages to connect the "huge looseness" of city life (116–17), and he is plainly mesmerized by the plenitude around him.

210. I am indebted to Elizabeth Long's work for helping me see this neglected aspect of the scholarly treatment of American culture. Elizabeth Long, *The American Dream and the Popular Novel* (London: Routledge & Kegan Paul, 1985), 148–90.

211. William H. Whyte, Jr., *The Organization Man* (New York: Simon and Schuster, 1956), 359–63.

212. David Riesman, with Nathan Glazer and Reuel Denney, *The Lonely Crowd: A Study of the Changing American Character* (New Haven: Yale University Press, 1961).

213. John D. MacDonald, *The Quick Red Fox* (New York: Ballantine, 1964), 167–68.

214. It seems to me unlikely that the "great awakening" of the 1960s could have happened at all if the 1950s were quite as conformist as critics insist. For the "native's" point of view, see the sometimes penetrating remarks from Freedman who sees the nonconformity in the conformity and vice versa. Morris Freedman, *Confessions of a*

pages 92–95 *Conformist* (New York: W.W. Norton & Company, 1961). Students of race, class, gender, and age during the period claimed to find diversity aplenty. A better notion has been proposed, that of "containment." This would help explain outward conformity and allow for diversity "within." See Andrew Ross, *No Respect: Intellectuals and Popular Culture* (New York: Routledge, 1989), and Alan Nadel, *Containment Culture: American Narratives, Postmodernism, and the Atomic Age* (Durham, NC: Duke University Press, 1996). But I believe even this idea is insufficient for it posits a monolithic, conspiratorial opponent to diversity. Nothing so organized was possible under the circumstances.

215. Northrop Frye, *The Modern Century* (Toronto: Oxford University Press, 1967), 36.

216. Daniel J. Boorstin, *The Americans: The Democratic Experience* (New York: Random House, 1973), 135, 411.

217. Christopher Lasch, *The Culture of Narcissism: American Life in an Age of Diminishing Expectations* (New York: W.W. Norton and Company, 1978), 66.

218. Elizabeth Long, *The American Dream and the Popular Novel* (London: Routledge & Kegan Paul, 1985) 165.

219. Daniel Bell, *The Cultural Contradictions of Capitalism* (New York: Basic Books, 1976).

220. Christopher Lasch, *The Culture of Narcissism: American Life in an Age of Diminishing Expectations* (New York: W.W. Norton and Company, 1978), xx. A more detailed criticism of this book will be offered in book 2 of the Culture by Commotion series.

221. I haven't made any explicit reference to the intellectuals' hostility for one of the most important and vital aspects of plenitude, the women's movement. This has been too well documented in the feminist literature to need repeating here.

222. Robert Fulford, "Age of Reason Eludes Heaven's Gate Cultists," *Globe and Mail*, 9 April 1997, E1. This "intellectual" plays a middle game in which he beards academics for not being journalistic enough and journalists for not being academic enough. This gives him ready-made criticism, and, always, a place to hide. For more on the inclination of the intellectual to explain plenitude as an example of the ravages of popular culture, see book 2 and the discussion of the film critic David Denby.

223. Mr. Fulford might wish to play the academic here and consult some of the literature on the topic: Lawrence Grossberg, "MTV: Swinging on a (Postmodern) Star," in *Cultural Politics in Contemporary America*, ed. Ian Angus and Suht Jhally (New York: Routledge, 1989); E. Ann Kaplan, *Rocking around the Clock: Music, Television, Post Modernism and Consumer Culture* (New York: Routledge, 1987); Lisa A. Lewis, *Gender Politics and MTV: Voicing the Difference* (Philadelphia: Temple University Press, 1990).

224. Weinstein has made award-winning videos for Jann Arden. Sigismondi made a remarkable video for Marilyn Manson and is, at this writing, at work on a David Bowie video.

225. Conrad Black is a press "baron" who owns a great many newspapers in England and North America. He is a conspicuous member of the Canadian Right. Rick Salutin is a playwright, academic, and journalist who writes for the *Globe and Mail* and speaks for some part of the Canadian Left. They are a perfectly matched pair to the extent they are both articulate, voluble, and unfailingly unoriginal.

226. Lynn Barber, *The Heyday of Natural History 1820–1870* (London: Jonathan Cape, 1980), 28, 30.

227. Paul Litt, "The Massey Commission, Americanization, and Canadian Cultural Nationalism," *Queen's Quarterly* 98, no. 2 (1991): 375–87.

228. Hilton Kramer is, of course, the tragically underachieving editor of *The New Critierion*.

229. Two excellent, general, accounts of complexity theory are available. I prefer the first. M. Mitchell Waldrop, *Complexity: The Emerging Science at the Edge of Order and Chaos* (New York: Simon and Schuster, 1992); Roger Lewin, *Complexity: Life at the Edge of Chaos* (New York: Macmillan, 1992).

230. Stuart Kauffman, qtd. in M. Mitchell Waldrop, *Complexity: The Emerging Science at the Edge of Order and Chaos* (New York: Simon and Schuster, 1992), 126.

231. Stuart Kauffman, qtd. in M. Mitchell Waldrop, *Complexity: The Emerging Science at the Edge of Order and Chaos* (New York: Simon and Schuster, 1992), 127.

232. There are too many examples for comprehensive review, but the work on process, ritual, structuration, performative theory, and *habitas* are germane. See Mikhail Bakhtin, *The Dialogic Imagination: Four Essays*, ed. Michael Holquist (Austin: University of Texas Press, 1981); Pierre Bourdieu, *The Logic of Practice*, trans. Richard Nice (Stanford: Stanford University Press, 1990); Anthony Giddens, *The Constitution of Society: Outline of the Theory of Structuration* (Berkeley: University of California Press, 1984); Nancy D. Munn, *The Fame of Gawa: A Symbolic Study of Value Transformation in a Massim Society* (New York: Cambridge University Press, 1986); Stanley Jeyaraja Tambiah, *Culture, Thought, and Social Action: An Anthropological Perspective* (Cambridge: Harvard University Press, 1985).

233. John Holland, qtd. in M. Mitchell Waldrop, *Complexity: The Emerging Science at the Edge of Order and Chaos* (New York: Simon and Schuster, 1992), 171, 254.

234. Chris Langton, qtd. in M. Mitchell Waldrop, *Complexity: The Emerging Science at the Edge of Order and Chaos* (New York: Simon and Schuster, 1992), 293.

235. Mike Brake, *Comparative Youth Culture: The Sociology of Youth Cultures and Youth Subcultures in America, Britain, and Canada* (London: Routledge & Kegan Paul, 1985), 8. The key text here is Dick Hebdige, *Subculture: The Meaning of Style* (New York: Methuen, 1979).

236. This is a distinction almost always elided by the Birmingham school.

237. Fredric Jameson, "Postmodernism and Consumer Society," in *The Anti-Aesthetic: Essays on Postmodern Culture*, ed. Hal Foster (Port Townsend, WA: Bay Press, 1983), 114.

238. Fredric Jameson, *Postmodernism, or, The Cultural Logic of Late Capitalism* (Durham, NC: Duke University Press, 1991), 323, 330.

239. Fredric Jameson, *Postmodernism, or, The Cultural Logic of Late Capitalism* (Durham, NC: Duke University Press, 1991), 18, 26. I believe this argument turns on a Nietzschean panic. When we say there is no absolute authenticity, surely we are not obliged to say that there are not degrees of authenticity. (Still more surely, we do not

pages 102–104 want to dispute the sense of authenticity experienced by the actor. See, for instance, Sue Widdicombe and Robin Woofitt, "'Being' versus 'Doing' Punk: On Achieving Authenticity as a Member," *Journal of Language and Social Psychology* 9 (1990), 257–77.) To discover that the continuum is not anchored in the "true true" and the "real real" does not mean that the continuum is indeed unthinkable or impracticable, nor, more to the anthropological point, that it does not satisfactorily inform the thoughts and emotions of millions of contemporary Westerners countless times a day. The postmodernists are perhaps too quick (too eager?) to take to the lifeboats. A version of this point may be found in Victor Burgin, *The End of Art Theory: Criticism and Postmodernity* (Atlantic Highlands, NJ: Humanities Press International, 1986), 198. See also Peter Dews, *The Limits of Disenchantment: Essays on Contemporary European Philosophy* (London: Verso, 1995).

240. G.W. Beattie, "Turn-Taking and Interruption in Political Interviews," *Semiotica* 39 (1982), 93–113. S. Duncan, "Some Signals and Rules for Taking Turns in Conversations," *Journal of Personality and Social Psychology* 23 (1972), 283–92. Bengt Orestrom, *Turn-Taking in English Conversation* (Lund: CWK Gleerup, 1983). Harvey Sacks, Emanuel A. Schegloff, and Gail Jefferson, "A Simplest Systematics for the Organization of Turn-Taking for Conversation," *Language* 50, no. 4 (1974), 696–735.

241. I leave for another occasion the still deeper contradiction in the postmodernist position. It may fairly be asked whether postmodernism could have established itself as an intellectual community (even as a fractious, heterogeneous community) if the world were what postmodernism says it is. If the world were truly a place of partial structures, exhausted narratives, empty signs, and endlessly heterogeneous discourse, how could a new idea, especially such a revolutionary one, have emerged and come to claim so many advocates, journals, departments, and grants. There is now a "culture" of postmodernism within and without the academic world. Strictly speaking, such a thing should be impossible.

242. Erving Goffman, *Behavior in Public Places* (New York: The Free Press, 1963). Erving Goffman, *Interaction Ritual* (New York: Anchor Books, 1967). Erving Goffman, *Relations in Public* (New York: Harper and Row, 1971). A good example of the importance of invisible rules comes in a paper by Charles Ferguson who, for study purposes, withheld his customary "good morning" from his secretary. "The second day was full of tension. I got strange looks [from everyone] and there was a definite air of 'what's wrong with Ferguson?' I abandoned the experiment on the third day because I was afraid of explosive and possibly lasting consequences." Charles A. Ferguson, "The Structure and Use of Politeness Formulas," *Language in Society* 5 (1976): 140.

243. Bourdieu's treatment of *habitas* is especially good on the transparency of culture: Pierre Bourdieu, *The Logic of Practice*, trans. Richard Nice (Stanford, CA: Stanford University Press, 1990).

244. I have treated Jameson as my "straw man." Characteristically, Baudrillard has some very interesting things to say on the topic, including that America is a "society of complexity, hybridity and the greatest intermingling." But this is for him a "superficial diversity." Certain differences are disappearing, including, mysteriously, the gender

one. He detects "an absence of difference, bound up with a decline in the display of sexual characteristics. The outer signs of masculinity are tending towards zero, but so are the signs of feminity" (Jean Baudrillard, *America*, trans. Chris Turner [London and New York: Verso, 1989], 7, 41.) We must wonder at the ethnographic veracity of this observation. Certainly, some groups are experiencing a kind of convergence, but for many others difference flourishes.

245. But see Ihab Hassan's suggestion that indeterminacy and a feeling for "openness, heterodoxy, pluralism, electicism, randomness, revolt, deformation" define postmodernism: Ihab Hassan, "Ideas of Cultural Change," in *Innovation/Renovation: New Perspectives on the Humanities*, ed. Ihab Hassan and Sally Hassan (Madison: University of Wisconsin Press, 1983), 27–28. Hassan may be rethinking this issue: Ihab Hassan, *Rumors of Change: Essays of Five Decades* (Tuscaloosa: Alabama University Press, 1995), xv-xvi.

246. Is this alliteration supposed to make it easier to remember? Gail Sheehy, *New Passages: Mapping Your Life across Time* (New York: Random House, 1995).

247. Michael Adams, *Sex in the Snow* (Toronto: Viking Canada, 1997).

248. Katharine Washburn and John F. Thorton, eds., *Dumbing Down: Essays on the Strip-Mining of American Culture* (New York: Norton, 1996).

249. For the best recent statement of the improvements in American television, see Robert Thompson, *Television's Second Golden Age: From 'Hill Street Blues' to 'Picket Fences'* (New York: Continuum, 1996). See also Bruce Handy, "Television: The Real Golden Age Is Now, *Time*, 30 October 1995, http://www.pathfinder.com/@@@ UxqRgQAJ8VAHt2p/time/magazine/domestic/1995/951030/television.html.

250. Dwight Macdonald, *Against the American Grain* (London: Gollancz, 1963).

251. *The Dukes of Hazzard* was a television comedy running on CBS from 1979 to 1985.

252. I acknowledge a contradiction: the following discussion uses the monolithic categories "Left" and "Right" and so fails to honour the notion of plenitude. But these great ideological tribes are still with us. They dictate other choices: opinion on diverse issues, reading material, friendship circles, clothing styles, leisure activities, even living room furnishings. Anyone who knows a young fogey or an old Marxist knows this to be true. But I use "Left" and "Right" with the understanding that the age of plenitude is upon us. Increasingly, we see people making their social, cultural, and political choices as if from a smorgasbord, mixing and matching these issues according not to the dictates of a single ideological position but their own diverse inclinations and beliefs.

253. Heather MacDonald, "The Sobol Report: Multiculturalism Triumphant," in *Against the Grain: The New Criterion on Art and Intellect at the End of the Twentieth Century*, ed. Hilton Kramer and Roger Kimball (Chicago: Ivan R. Dee, 1995), 109–22.

254. It is interesting to observe, for instance, how often DeParle doubts and diminishes the motives of players on the Christian right in his recent *New York Times* piece. Jason DeParle, "A Fundamental Problem," *New York Times Magazine*, 14 July 1996, 18–25, 32, 38, 42, 44.

255. Pat Robertson, qtd. in Jason DeParle, "A Fundamental Problem," *New York Times Magazine*, 14 July 1996, 24.

Culture by Commotion

256. David W. Dunlap, "Gay Advertising Campaign on TV Draws Wrath of Conservatives," *New York Times*, 12 November 1995, Y15.

257. James Bennet, "Patrick J. Buchanan: Candidate's Speech Is Called Code for Controversy," *New York Times*, 25 February 1996, 15. This *is* a speech convention of the racist. For one racist's practice of calling all African Americans "George," see Henry Louis Gates, Jr., *Loose Canons: Notes on the Culture Wars* (New York: Oxford University Press, 1992), 133, whose father was so called.

258. Erich Goode and Ben-Yehuda Nachman, *Moral Panics: The Social Construction of Deviance* (Oxford: Blackwell, 1994). I make this point not because the Right needs (or welcomes) my advice but to show that plenitude is so little understood by the Right it is prepared to contradict its own self-interest.

259. There is a large and turbulent body of debate on how inclusive Western societies have proven to be (see, for instance, William A. Gamson, *The Strategy of Social Protest*, 2d ed. [Belmont, CA: Wadsworth, 1990]). Two things are clear: seen comparatively, these societies have been more inclusive than other cultural traditions, and seen internally, they have never been inclusive enough. Western societies have always been more generative of difference than inclusive of it.

260. William J. Bennett, *The De-valuing of America: The Fight for Our Culture and Our Children* (New York: Summit Books, 1992), 32, 33.

261. Arnold van Gennep, *The Rites of Passage*, trans. Monika B. Vizedom and Gabrielle L. Caffee (Chicago: University of Chicago Press, 1960).

262. Tocqueville paid careful attention to this theme and it is well observed in Frances Fitzgerald, "Sun City" (1983), in *Cities on a Hill: A Journey through Contemporary American Cultures* (New York: Touchstone, Simon and Schuster, 1987), and Lindsy Van Gelder and Pamela Robin Brandt, *The Girls Next Door: Into the Heart of Lesbian America* (New York: Simon and Schuster, 1996).

263. Matei Calinescu, "From the One to the Many: Pluralism in Today's Thought," in Hassan and Hassan, *Innovation/Renovation*, 268. The full Booth reference: Wayne C. Booth, *Critical Understanding: The Powers and Limits of Pluralism* (Chicago: University of Chicago Press, 1979).

264. Ernest Gellner, introduction to *Notions of Nationalism*, ed. Sukumar Periwal (Budapest: Central European University Press, 1995), 2.

265. I believe this is true even of the best ethnographies to emerge from the Birmingham school.

266. See http://www.lib.umich.edu/libhome/services/diverslib.html.

267. George Wolfe, interview by bell hooks, *Bomb*, Winter 1995, 48; emphasis added.

268. Kristal Brent Zook, "A Manifesto of Sorts for a Black Feminist Movement," *New York Times Magazine*, 12 November 1995, 89.

269. Todd Gitlin, "The Rise of Identity Politics," *Dissent*, Spring 1993, 172–77. See also Neil Bissoondath, *Selling Illusions* (Toronto: Penguin Books, 1994).

270. See, for instance, William V. Spanos, *The End of Education: Toward Posthumanism* (Minneapolis: University of Minneapolis Press, 1993), and Cheryl Zarlenga Kerchis and Iris Marion Young, "Social Movements and the Politics of Difference," in

271. The following discussion is indebted in several ways to the extraordinary works of Daniel Bell and Marshall Sahlins.

272. This is a little too summary, perhaps. There is a transformational chain in our culture of the following stages: Labour creates soap. Soap in turn becomes a creator of and a symbol of parental solicitude. Solicitude is then seized upon in the construction of "gender" as a peculiarly female thing to display and distribute. Now solicitude has been gendered and women constructed. This gendering of the world helps construct it. Out of this and other cultural notions we create an entire society—which then demands, constructs, distributes, and constructs "soap" that the cycle might begin all over again.

273. I evoke the tower of babel not as the intellectuals usually do, as a warning against the collapse of meaning, but to acknowledge that as the world becomes more multiple and various we will need institutions that are "roomy" enough to accommodate this multiplicity and diversity. This is, I hope, not quite the same as saying we have lost our way, that our institutions are in disarray, and that our only hope is to damn popular culture and return to orthodoxy. This response helps create the crisis it claims to warn us against.

274. Andreas Huyssen, *Twilight Memories: Marking Time in a Culture of Amnesia* (New York: Routledge, 1995).

275. Linnaeus (1707–1778) was a Swede, a professor of medicine and botany at the University of Uppsala, and the author of *Species Plantarum* (1753) and *Systema Naturae* (1758) which established the foundations of modern botanical and zoological classification. In a sense, Linnaeus was a biblical presence, a second Adam, supplying a language with which nature could be named and scrutinized.

Culture by Commoti

276. Lynn Barber, *The Heyday of Natural History 1820–1870* (London: Jonathan Cape, 1980), 33–43. My account here is more evocative than exacting. For an example of the latter, see the exemplary Mary P. Winsor, *Reading the Shape of Nature: Comparative Zoology at the Agassiz Museum* (Chicago: University of Chicago Press, 1991).

277. Lynn Barber, *The Heyday of Natural History 1820–1870* (London: Jonathan Cape, 1980), 13.

278. The questions here are simple ones: Can we create a study of 20th-century plenitude that is not objectifying, patronizing, and controlling? Can we recapture the superbly disinterested spirit of some Victorian study and jettison its inclination to colonize the field of knowledge?

279. Jonathan Raban, *Old Glory: An American Voyage* (New York: Simon and Schuster, 1981). Bill Bryson, *The Lost Continent: Travels in Small Town America* (New York: Harper & Row, 1989).

280. John James Audubon (1785–1851) was the author of the extraordinary *Birds of America, 1827–1838*, and easily the greatest of the artists who made this their topic. The 19th century awarded the term "genius" perhaps more generously than we do in the 20th century. Audubon would have earned it in either century.

281. Edward Said, *Orientalism* (New York: Pantheon Books, 1978).

pages 129—130 282. Lewis Henry Morgan, *Systems of Consanguinity and Affinity of the Human Family* (Oosterhout, NB: Anthropological Publications, 1970). Sir James Augustus Henry Murray, Henry Bradley, Sir William A. Craigie, C.T. Onions, Philological Society (Great Britain), and Birdsall & Son, *A New English Dictionary on Historical Principles: Founded Mainly on the Materials Collected by the Philological Society* (Oxford: Clarendon Press, 1888–1933). Sir Leslie Stephen and Sir Sidney Lee, *Dictionary of National Biography* (New York: Macmillan, 1885–1900).

283. This topic is treated in more detail above in the section entitled "Plenitude's Fellow Travellers."

284. Peter Wake, "Goths: Frequently Asked Questions," http://www.cis.ohio-state.edu/hypertext/faq/usenet/gothic-faq/faq.html and Stephen Martin, "Dear Doc Marten: Questions and Answers about the Skinhead Subculture," http://www.geocities.com/CapitolHill/Lobby/2231/ddm.html.

285. See his rave Web site and FAQ (http://www.hyperreal.com/raves/altraveFAQ.html) at http://www.hyperreal.com: "I am MORE than happy to incorporate others' suggestions into the FAQ, to include dissenting opinions and statements." See also http://www.hyperreal.com/~mike/pub/altraveFAQ.html.

286. James Clifford and George E. Marcus, *Writing Culture: The Poetics and Politics of Ethnography* (Berkeley: University of California Press, 1986). Linda Hutcheon, *The Politics of Representation in Canadian Art and Literature* (Toronto: York University, 1988).

287. http://www.alt.culture.com/site/entries-text. See also the print version: Nathaniel Wice and Steven Daly, *Alt.culture: An A-to-Z Guide to the '90s — Underground, On-line, and Over-the-Counter* (New York: HarperPerennial, 1995).

ACKNOWLEDGEMENTS

Thanks are due to the following: Lynn Appleby (Appleby Design), David Barr (Royal Ontario Museum), Jill Batson (Spoken Word), Dennis Baxter (CIBC), Jeanne Beker (*FashionTelevision*, CITY-TV), Russell Belk (University of Utah), Hargurchet Bhabra (TVOntario), Gloria Bishop (Canadian Broadcasting Corporation), Sandra Boekholt (University of Amsterdam), Patrick Bova (National Opinion Research Center Library), Jeff Brown (University of Toronto), Ronnie Burbank (Royal Ontario Museum), Naomi Buck (York University), Anne Cameron (Royal Ontario Museum), Sagrario Castilla (The Studio), James Chatto (*Toronto Life*), Cindy Clark (C.D. Clark, Ltd.), Howard Collinson (Royal Ontario Museum), Robin Chow (Xbase), Chris Commins (Commins Wingrove), Susan Cook (Book City, Toronto), Amy Craig (Harpo Productions), Pat Crane (Eastman Kodak, Rochester), John Cruickshank (*Vancouver Sun*), Aaron Dawe (Burn Jane Burn), John Dalla Costa, Jim and Laima Dingwell (Vancouver), Linda Dunlop (Canadian Broadcasting Corporation, now TVOntario), Gwynne Dyer (London), Elena Escalona (Mexico City), Tim Falconer (Toronto), Gerry Flahive (National Film Board), Marnie Fleming (Oakville Galleries), David Fogel (Adobe Systems), Robert Fulford (*Globe and Mail*), Rachel Giese (*Xtra Magazine*), Robert Glossop (The Vanier Institute of the Family), Cynthia Good (Penguin Canada), Rodney Graham (Vancouver), Robert Gray (Commins Wingrove), Casey Greer (University of Utah), Julia Harrison (University of Trent), Peter Herrndorf (TVOntario), Adrienne Hood (University of Toronto), Colleen Humer, Rita Johnson (Royal Ontario Museum), Bill Johnstone, M.D. (Toronto), Ivan Kalmar (University of Toronto), Irmi Karl (University of Sussex), Katherine Kay (Stikeman, Elliot), Jim King (Research International), Mark Kingwell (University of Toronto), Bob Kincaide (Hazelton Group), Shirley Knott (*Globe and Mail*), Nadine Kriston (*Shift Magazine*), Joan Kron (*Allure Magazine*), Peter, Julian and Elisabeth Laywine, Beverly Lemire (University of New Brunswick), Sue Leonard (The Ongoing Partnership), Anne Lewison (Pei Cobb Fried and Partners), Mike Lotti (Eastman Kodak, Rochester), Tom Luke (Bozell Worldwide), Debra Luneau (Royal Ontario Museum), Andy Macaulay (Roche, Macaulay and Partners), Margaret Mark (Young and Rubicam), Sid McCusker (Victoria), Jim McKenna (McKenna Productions), Scott McKenzie (CIBC), Barnaby Marshall (*Shift Magazine*), Anne Martin-Matthews (University of Guelph), Julia Matthews (Library, Royal Ontario Museum), Glenn David Mick (University of Wisconsin), Alan Middleton (York University, Toronto), Mary Mills (JWT), Scott Mitchell,

Heather Monroe Blum (University of Toronto), Will Novosedlik (Russell, Inc.), Catherine O'Hara (Canadian Broadcasting Corporation), Annie Pedret (MIT), Debra Perna (psdesign), Cecelia Potter (Toronto), John Prevost (Avon Corporation), Rita Rayman (Toronto), Gilbert Reid (Toronto), Elizabeth Renzetti (*Globe and Mail*), Geoffrey Roche (Roche, Macaulay and Partners), Paula Rosch (Kimberley Clark), Chris Sasaki (Planetarium), Charles Saumerez Smith (National Portrait Gallery), Hans-Dieter Seus (Royal Ontario Museum), Eric Siegrist (psdesign), Lee Simpson (Maclean Hunter Publishers), John Sherry (Northwestern University), Sydney Smart, M.D., Jay Smith (Wood Gundy), Evan Solomon (*Shift Magazine*), Jim Stacey (Magnum Communications), Bill Stern (*LA Weekly*), Diana Stinson (Toronto), Richard Stursberg (Canadian Cable Television Association), Dr. Lynn Thurling, M.D., Elizabeth Torlee (Bozell Palmer Bonner), Wodek Szemberg (TVOntario), Loretta Yarlow (Art Gallery of York University), Khalil Younes (KO, Budapest), Wentworth Walker (Toronto), Margot Welch (Royal Ontario Museum), Wendy Weisner (Stentor), Tim Wingrove (Commins Wingrove), Rick Wolfe (PostStone Corporation), Eberhard Zeidler (Zeidler Roberts Partnership), Philip Zimmerman (New-York Historical Society), Moses Znaimer (CITY-TV) and Sergio Zyman (Coca-Cola Company). Special thanks to the past Director of the Royal Ontario Museum, Dr. John McNeill, and especially the present one, Dr. Lindsay Sharp. Special thanks to the Department of Anthropology at the Royal Ontario Museum for putting me up (and putting up with me) while I was writing this book: Mima Kapches, Arnie Brownstone, (the endlessly patient and knowledgeable) Ronnie Burbank, Liz Graham, Ken Lister, Trudy Nicks, David Pendergast, and Angela Raljic. Special thanks to Dave Dyment for instruction in contemporary art and music, to Julia Matthews and the staff of the Library and Archives of the Royal Ontario Museum for much help and many suggestions, to Alison Hahn and Nigel Smith (Hahn Smith Design) for their intelligence and sensitivity in the design of the Culture by Commotion series, and to the following people for serving as readers of the manuscript: Hargurchet Bhabra, Gloria Bishop, Jeff Brown, Laurie Brown, Dave Dyment, Marnie Fleming, Rachel Giese, Adrienne Hood, Anne Lewison, Julia Matthews, Alan Middleton, Heather Monroe Blum, Annie Pedret, Gilbert Reid, Evan Solomon, Suzanne Stein, Wodek Szemberg, Elizabeth Torlee, Wentworth Walker, Margot Welch, and Eberhard Zeidler. The book is better for their comments, criticisms, and encouragement. (Naturally, all faults and errors remain my own.) ❧

Designed by Hahn Smith Design, Toronto
Copyedited by Scott Mitchell
Typeset by Richard Hunt at Archetype
in Sabon, Beton and Whirlygig
Front cover & endpaper illustration
by Alison Hahn based on archival photographs
from the Library and Archives at
the Royal Ontario Museum
Printed on Mohawk Vellum
by Bowne of Toronto

Culture by Commotion
Forthcoming in the series
Book 2: Transformation
Book 3: Commotion